# Praise for *Leaders Are Born To Be Made*

"Many of the most valuable leadership lessons CEOs learn throughout their careers come from mistakes we have made along the way, the setbacks and hard-won triumphs that have helped us in our ongoing pursuit of becoming better leaders. I wish I had had Dr. Deptula's *Leaders Are Born To Be Made* actionable steps long ago. If you're serious about being a better leader, start here."

**—Sam Reese, CEO, Vistage Worldwide, Inc.**

"Remember, it is ALWAYS about the people. If you don't invest in your team, you can't succeed. Bryan presents a methodology to build leaders who can deliver results."

**—Bruce D. Werner, Strategic Advisor to Private Businesses, author *Your Ownership Journey***

"Bryan Deptula's book, *Leaders Are Born To Be Made*, succeeds where other leadership development books fail. The focus on self-leadership first is a refreshing approach to ensuring that leaders are well prepared to lead others. He demystifies the research on leadership and translates the evidence into clear guidelines. The book builds a solid foundation for improving leader-member relationships in the workplace."

**—Terri A. Scandura, Professor of Management, Academic Director, University of Miami**

"Dr. Deptula's work can best be described as a leadership manifesto. His truthful and unvarnished approach to learning actionable leadership skills is revolutionary. According to Manila Recruitment, employee turnover is caused by ten reasons. At the top of the list is 'bad bosses.' The truth works, all the time! *Leaders Are Born To Be Made* will help trainers, mentors, leaders, and aspiring leaders address eight of the top ten reasons for leadership failure."

**—J. Preston Jones, D.B.A.**

# LEADERS

## ARE BORN

## TO BE MADE

# LEADERS

# ARE BORN

# TO BE MADE

Practical wisdom from scientific journals on applied
psychology, leadership, and organizational behavior

**Proven Low-Risk, High-Reward
Ways To Make Executives And
Managers Better Leaders**

# BRYAN DEPTULA, MBA, PHD

INDIE BOOKS
INTERNATIONAL

The 3L Mission™ and Leader M.U.S.C.L.E.™ are pending trademarks of Bryan Deptula.
FIFA World Cup® is a registered trademark of Fédération Internationale de Football Association
Quantified Communications® is a registered trademark of Quantified.ai
Receptiviti® is a registered trademark of Receptiviti, Inc
Grammarly Business® is a registered trademark of Grammarly, Inc.
Docebo® is a registered trademark of Docebo, S.P.A.
EdCast® is a registered trademark of EdCast, Inc.
IBM® and Watson® are registered trademarks of International Business Machines Corporation
Shaping Tomorrow® is a registered trademark of Fujitsu Limited
Quid® is a registered trademark of Quid, LLC
15Five® is a registered trademark of 15Five, Inc.
Lattice® is a registered trademark of Lattice, Inc.
Viva Glint™ is a pending trademark of Microsoft Corporation
Qualtrics® is a registered trademark of Qualtrics, LLC
Enboarder® is a registered trademark of Enboard.me Pty Ltd
Click Boarding® is a registered trademark of Click Boarding, LLC
Degreed® is a registered trademark of Degreed, Inc.
Pluralsight Skills® is a registered trademark of Multivision Newco, LLC.
Marlboro Reds® is a registered trademark of Philip Morris USA Inc.
Zippo® is a registered trademark of Zippo Manufacturing Company
EZ-Widers® is a registered trademark of Republic Technologies (NA) LLC
Black Label® is a registered trademark of Pabst Brewing Company LLC
React® is a registered trademark of DataDirect Networks, Inc.
Django® is a registered trademark of Django Software Foundation
Fortune 500® and Fortune 100® are registered trademarks of Fortune Media IP Limited
PowerPoint® is a registered trademark of Microsoft Corporation
Gatorade® is a registered trademark of Stokely-Van Camp, Inc.

ISBN-13: 978-1-957651-97-2
Library of Congress Control Number: 2024922469

Designed by The BookDesigners

INDIE BOOKS INTERNATIONAL®, INC.
2511 WOODLANDS WAY
OCEANSIDE, CA 92054
www.indiebooksintl.com

# DEDICATION

I dedicate this testimony about my life to my loving wife, Kristen, and our children. My deepest appreciation to Kristen for enduring years of selfless dedication while supporting me throughout my MBA and PhD programs. In low times, she carried me, shared loving words, and offered motivating thoughts. In success, she celebrated my victories.

To Kristen: You're the one truth and my partner for life. I've loved you since the first time my eyes gazed upon your light. Thank you for taking this ride with me, supporting my wacky ideas, and being my everything.

To my children: Being born is the single greatest miracle any human being experiences. To be transported from your mother's womb out into the big wide world and to make it healthfully can only be achieved through God's blessings.

Nothing was ever the same after you were born, Gordon, and after you, Bryna. It never will be and was never intended to be the same because now everything is complete with you in our lives.

Gordon: I love how you cackle when you laugh so hard and tell me the pure joy of life you're experiencing in the infectious, deep belly laugh.

Bryna: Your hugs take me to a place of complete warmth and comfort, deep inside my soul, that lets me know your total affection for me. When you look at me and say, "Hi, Dad. I love you," this is the everything all humans should feel.

# CONTENTS

# PREFACE

## Why You Should Read This Book

Ah. Ah. Choo. The sneeze that changed everything.

The sound reverberated through the bar like a gunshot, freezing time itself. Isabella's sneeze exploded across our tiny table; a microscopic missile launch that sent us all diving for cover. Saliva droplets arced through the air like deadly comets. Everyone at the table contorted their bodies to avoid the deadly spittle.

November 2020. Rehoboth Beach, Delaware. COVID-19 pandemic in full effect. The world had become a place where a single sneeze could end lives, shutter businesses, and tear families apart.

As Isabella's face drained of color, her trembling hands clutching her phone, she announced a damning COVID-19-positive test result. Panic filled the hearts and minds of everyone at the table. Prior to that moment, my wife Kristen and I had done everything possible to avoid catching COVID-19.

Months of social isolation and staying six feet away from all other humans apart from immediate family, a wasted effort. Now, in a predictable but unanticipated event, my friend Isabella had sneezed directly into my face. Fear. Anxiety. Holy shit.

"Kristen," I choked out, "I've been exposed. I need to quarantine." With the contents of my mobile quarantine unit in my possession, I set up my tent on the frozen ground of the Indian River Inlet Bridge campground.

And so began my exile. Five nights of bone-chilling cold and soul-crushing isolation, followed by nine more nights in a sterile condo. Fourteen days to contemplate how I, Dr. Bryan

Deptula—once a globe-trotting leadership expert and new hotel owner—found myself sleeping under a bridge.

Just over a year before, in September 2019, Kristen and I had taken the biggest gamble of our lives, emptied our savings, leveraged our every asset, and accepted a "gift" from my mother to purchase the Canalside Inn. It was our dream to buy a hotel, convert it into a retreat center, and give me a platform to do the work God put me on this planet to do...pull the leader out from within every human being. I would deliver life-changing leadership workshops for companies and to the public. Guests would stay in our lodging rooms at night, take my courses and workshops in the day, and do team-building activities.

How could we have known that just months later, in early 2020, news of COVID-19 would cause the world to grind to a halt? The sudden pandemic and lockdown were a major blow to our business. We explored options for virtual conferences and online workshops, but companies weren't investing in leader development programs and people were literally banned from traveling. On April 6, 2020, the State of Delaware placed "Bans all short-term rental units—including vacation home rentals, hotels, motels, and condo rentals..." meaning that no guests except first responders and medical staff were permitted at any lodging facility.

As a couple, we were terrified that the risk we had taken would result in bankruptcy. We struggled to cope with the financial and emotional toll of the lockdown. The stress of operating our multimillion-dollar investment with no money, empty seminar rooms, deserted guest accommodations, and no end in sight to the lockdown made me want to throw up.

As I sat in that tent, freezing my ass off, mad at the world, I wondered how my life had led me to this moment. Early in 2019, life was "good" and going according to plan, and the world seemed "normal." In those days, I could use all the knowledge, skills, and abilities that I had acquired over my years of earning a Master of Business Administration (MBA) and a doctor of philosophy (PhD) in leadership and organizational behavior, and all my experience being a corporate trainer, executive, and professor to teach people everything I "knew" about how to be a leader. I had just been promoted to associate professor at Nova Southeastern University (NSU) and had also been nominated to—and accepted—the role of acting department chair for the Management Department in the College of Business. If that weren't enough, we were operating our leader development company, BKD Leaders, with much success. I was traveling around the country speaking to large crowds at packed conferences and corporate headquarters. I was speaking so much that I'd often call Kristen to ask what city I had woken up in and who the audience was for the day. It was common for me to be in front of a thousand people a month between my university graduate students, corporate clients, and conferences.

Looking in front of me at whitecaps atop the waves crashing on the beach, I reflected on my present circumstances, how the conditions of the world had forced me to lead our team of employees in ways that were new—as in how do you staff a hotel with a front desk person who is supposed to be the first point of contact with guests, when guests now demanded a "contactless experience?" How can we leverage technology to operate our hotel remotely—without being in person to greet guests—while maintaining the same level of customer satisfaction? How can we possibly meet the legal requirements and constantly changing health recommendations, while trying to accommodate one guest who wants us to sterilize every surface and wear masks behind a plastic barrier, when another guest comes in with no mask and close-talks every person in the lobby? It was on me to find solutions and lead in ways that I had never thought of. Here I was, a literal academic researcher and corporate trainer, at my wit's end about how to lead, utterly confused about what to do and how to do it. Somehow, after all that schooling and all the years as an executive, I was learning to lead again for the first time.

As I huddled in that tent, a revelation struck me: Everyone was learning to lead again, because everything we knew about leadership had to be applied in ways that we never imagined. Nobody knew what they were doing. We're all in this clusterfuck together, so we'd better figure out how to live and lead better such that we might get ourselves as expeditiously as possible back to a (new) normal.

The pandemic wasn't just a health crisis; it was a workplace transformation. Executives, once the masters of their corporate domains, were now adrift in the uncharted waters of remote work. Their once-unshakeable egos, mine included, gave way to a profound fear as they grappled with the unfamiliar challenges of leading virtual teams. Trust in leaders, governments, coworkers, and teammates eroded, productivity vanished, and once-solid businesses went out of business.

The pandemic only accelerated an already-in-progress work-from-home remote revolution. Leaders were forced to accept that some jobs required people to be in person, while other jobs be done from anywhere in the world. Leading in person as opposed to remotely requires different skill sets. Leadership fundamentals didn't need to change, only how you applied those skills—and through which medium you communicated—shifted like tectonic plates.

It's impossible to lead a team scattered across the globe using the same old-school prepandemic style, because if you do, you are begging for underperformance, resentment, and employee exodus. Companies clinging to traditional hierarchical structures and authoritarian leadership styles were significantly more likely to experience employee burnout, disengagement, and turnover during the pandemic. When leaders aren't adapting to their needs, employees recognize that their leaders suck. My takeaway was that people need to figure out who they are as leaders in this new reality, to learn new ways of leading, and to take leadership fundamentals and apply them in ways so that employees will respond positively.

Hallucinating from the dehydration of not drinking water and spending days alone outside in the cold, I saw a robot executive with metal hands leading legions of droids who had taken over all the human jobs. *Oh no.* Terminator *was a prophecy.* Rise of the Machines *is real!* After snapping out of that technophobia psychosis panic attack, it occurred to me that the rise of artificial intelligence (AI) caused fears in others. As AI systems became increasingly sophisticated, they began to automate tasks once exclusive to humans, forcing leaders to confront the very nature of their work.

World Economic Forum Annual Report 2022–2023 calls for a "reskilling revolution," emphasizing that "Technological shifts, geo-economic pressures, demographic changes and the green transition are creating structural churn across jobs and skills. Preparing learners and workers to navigate and thrive through this disruption is key to ensuring economic prosperity, social mobility, and societal stability." According to the Forum's Future of Jobs Report 2023, almost a quarter of jobs (23 percent) are expected to change in the next five years and over 40 percent of the core skills needed in the average job are also expected to change. This report is not the sci-fi fiction stuff of spaceships and aliens; this is real science that real people fear could take their jobs—their livelihoods—and food off their family table. AI stirs up fear because its impacts are unknown, and the unknown is scary. Leaders, you must learn how to leverage AI to make yourselves better leaders.

Around the tenth day of quarantine, sick and tired of blowing kisses to my wife and children from ten feet away, I started thinking about my TEDx Talk *Leaders Are Born To Be Made.* In that TEDx Talk, I made (and I continue to make) the bold assertion that every person is capable of being a leader. All the research answering the question, "Are leaders born or made?" points to biological and DNA evidence that yes, some people are natural born leaders and some people are not; but DNA is not destiny. I'm not suggesting that every person has the potential to become a CEO, just that everyone has a moment when it's their time to lead, and we'd better prepare them to perform well when it is their turn.

The most profound shift in understanding leadership is emerging from looking inside the brain at the neurological level. Research in neuroscience has shown that the constant bombardment of digital stimuli is reshaping our brains, shortening our attention spans, and rewiring our neural pathways. This has profound implications for leadership, as it requires a fundamental rethinking of how we communicate, motivate, and inspire others.

Neuroleadership shows how by aligning your leadership with the way your brain naturally functions, you can create an environment that literally makes your team's brains light up with enthusiasm and productivity. Positive leadership—think praise, rewards, or a boss who genuinely has your back—causes your brain to release a cocktail of "happiness hormones" (dopamine, serotonin, and oxytocin) that trigger motivation and engagement. Conversely, dealing with a nightmare boss or a toxic work environment triggers your brain's stress response and releases cortisol.

The pandemic forced us to confront a harsh truth: We had become weak leaders who relied on familiar tactics that made us feel strong but were ill-suited for the challenges of the twenty-first century. Clinging to outdated leadership models no longer serves us. The very tools that once propelled us to success are now holding us back. Our once-powerful leadership muscles are now weak. We need to develop new leadership muscles, to master the art of asynchronous communication, virtual trust-building, and remote performance management.

Tucked into a windblown tent, alone with my thoughts, I realized that for my entire life—from my academic pursuits to my entrepreneurial ventures—I had been preparing for this moment, to share with the world low-risk/high-reward ways to make managers and executives better leaders.

But how?

The world needs a new approach to leadership, one that acknowledges the profound changes we are experiencing at a biological, psychological, and societal level. We must embrace the discomfort of growth, the challenge of learning new ways of leading.

My life's mission is to encourage human beings to lead and offer them proper nutrition (food for thought in this book) and exercises (application strategies) to build Leader M.U.S.C.L.E. (which I will define in the next section), to become leaders worth following. I offer you a memoir and research-backed instructive account of how to become your future best self and learn why some people are "natural born leaders" while others take a lifetime to evolve into leaders.

This is a fundamental shift in how we cultivate the leaders of tomorrow. It's a reimagining of leader development that acknowledges the intricate dance among our biology, the ever-present force of technology, and the vast potential within each leader. This is a call to change the way people live and lead.

This book serves two primary purposes. First, it offers an instructive model for you to evolve into your future best-leader self. Second, it contextualizes present-day leadership challenges, including leading postpandemic, leveraging AI to become a better leader, and offering insight into neuroleadership. You'll get actionable strategies to become a leader that serves not just the bottom line by driving performance, but also helps you find your path to wholeness and self-leadership.

Each section contains chapters that tell a purposeful story, culminating in a lesson about life and how those experiences led to personal growth that catapulted my evolution into a leader. Every story is designed to elaborate a leadership lesson grounded in the science of leading. There are zero nonsensical, unsubstantiated information or recommendations.

Within these pages, you'll find a deep dive into your unique leadership profile. We'll analyze your experiences, challenge your assumptions, and uncover the potential that makes you a one-of-a-kind leader. Through real-world examples, you'll gain insights into your leadership style, strengths, and areas for growth. To start again as an effective and enduring leader in today's world, you must deeply understand your leadership self-concept, continuously adapt to your environment, and evolve both personally and professionally to meet the ever-changing challenges of the present day. You write your own leadership journey and work toward being the type of leader that fits your life.

# INTRODUCTION

## Building Leader M.U.S.C.L.E. Model

*Leaders Are Born To Be Made*, the book, presents my Leader M.U.S.C.L.E. model. This model includes the most critical elements for leadership excellence, organizational productivity, and individual well-being. Leader M.U.S.C.L.E. was developed through extensive proprietary research and real-world application and is a proven training program used by thousands of employees worldwide across diverse industries and company sizes. It empowers leaders to navigate the complexities of the post-pandemic conditions to create a healthy, productive leadership practice.

Here's a simple way to think about the model:

## M = ME (Accepting That "All Leadership Starts With Me")

The journey of leadership begins with a deep understanding of yourself. This foundational pillar of the M.U.S.C.L.E. model emphasizes the importance of self-awareness, personal growth, and the development of a strong leader identity.

- *Leaders Are Born To Be Made—Understanding The Biology, Neurology, DNA, And Motivation To Lead*: People's unique genetic makeup influences who is more and less likely to be perceived as a natural leader. But, leadership is a skill that can be taught and learned, meaning that every person is capable of leading. Chan and Drasgow defined motivation to lead (MTL) as an individual difference construct that influences a person's decisions to assume leadership roles, training, and responsibilities, as well as their intensity of effort and persistence in leading.

- *Leader Identity And Brand*: Leader identity refers to the meaning you attach to yourself in relation to others when you are in a leadership role, specific to each relationship and context. It is the part of your overall self-concept specific to leadership. Your leadership brand conveys your identity and distinctiveness as a leader. Personal branding is the process of establishing your image and value in the minds of others. A strong personal leadership brand amplifies what's powerful and effective about your leadership, enabling you to generate maximum value. A leader's purpose consists of the central motivating goals for being a leader. This purpose guides actions and inspires others.

- *Self-Leadership*: The ability to manage one's emotions, behaviors, and thoughts is crucial for effective leadership. Self-leadership enables you to influence yourself, make sound decisions, and navigate challenges with resilience.

## U = UNDERSTANDING (Leader Intelligence)

Leader intelligence refers to the cognitive and emotional abilities that enable individuals to effectively guide, inspire, and influence others toward a common goal. It encompasses a wide range of skills, including critical thinking, creative thinking and strategic thinking, adaptability, interpersonal skills, learning agility, systems thinking, and ethical decision-making. Effective leaders possess a keen understanding of their environment, their team, and the dynamics of the modern workplace. This section of the M.U.S.C.L.E. model explores the various facets of leader intelligence required to thrive in the postpandemic era:

- *Leadership Styles*: Leaders must be adaptable, drawing from a variety of styles (transformational, transactional, servant, charismatic) to suit different situations and individuals.

- *Artificial Intelligence*: Leaders should embrace AI as a tool to enhance decision-making, streamline processes, and personalize learning. AI can significantly improve employee performance and reduce training costs, but it cannot replace essential human leadership skills like strategic thinking, empathy, and ethical decision-making.

## S = STRATEGY (Vision, Mission, Values, And ABCV: Always Be Creating Value)

Leadership is not just about managing the present; it's about shaping the future. The strategizing pillar of the M.U.S.C.L.E. model emphasizes the importance of creating a compelling vision, defining a clear mission, and upholding core values, all while continuously creating value (ABCV).

- *Vision*: A leader's vision is a vivid and inspiring picture of a desired future state. It provides direction, motivates action, and aligns the efforts of individuals and teams throughout the organization. A shared vision fosters a sense of purpose and collective commitment.

- *Mission*: A mission statement is a concise declaration of an organization's core purpose and reason for existence. It answers the fundamental question, "How and why do we do what we do?" A clear and meaningful mission statement guides decision-making, attracts talent, and builds a strong organizational culture.

- *Values*: Values are the deeply held beliefs and principles that guide an organization's behavior and decision-making. They serve as a moral compass, ensuring that actions are consistent with the organization's core identity and ethical standards.

- *ABCV (Always Be Creating Value)*: Leaders must instill a mindset of continuous value creation. This means constantly seeking ways to innovate, improve, and deliver greater value to customers, employees, and stakeholders. By embracing ABCV, leaders foster a culture of continuous improvement, where experimentation and risk-taking are encouraged.

## C = CONFLICT (How To Use Conflict To Generate Win-Win Solutions)

Conflict is an inherent part of human interaction, and it's no different in the workplace. However, conflict doesn't have to be destructive. The conflict pillar of the M.U.S.C.L.E. model emphasizes that conflict, when managed effectively, can be a catalyst for growth, innovation, and stronger relationships.

- *Win-Win Solutions*: Leaders skilled in conflict resolution aim to find solutions that benefit all parties involved. This involves active listening, empathy, open communication, and a willingness to compromise. By seeking win-win outcomes, leaders build trust, foster collaboration, and resolve conflicts in a way that strengthens relationships.

- *Innovation*: Conflict can spark creativity and lead to breakthrough ideas. By encouraging diverse perspectives and constructive debate, leaders can harness the energy of conflict to drive innovation and solve complex problems.

- *Building Relationships*: Conflict can be an opportunity to deepen understanding and empathy among individuals and teams. When handled with respect and a focus on mutual understanding, conflict can lead to stronger bonds and a more cohesive workplace culture.

- *Difficult Conversations*: Leaders must be willing to have challenging conversations when necessary. By addressing issues directly and honestly, they prevent conflicts from escalating and create a culture of trust and accountability.

## L = LEARNING (How To Be A Mentor And Learn Every Day)

Learning is a lifelong endeavor, and leaders must be committed to continuous growth and development. The learning pillar of the M.U.S.C.L.E. model emphasizes the importance of mentorship, adapting to new technologies, and embracing a learner's mindset.

- *Mentoring*: Mentoring is a powerful tool for leadership development. Leaders have a responsibility to share their wisdom, knowledge, and experience with others, guiding and supporting aspiring leaders on their own journeys. Mentoring relationships benefit both the mentor and mentee, fostering growth, learning, and mutual respect.

- *Making Life-Changing Decisions*: Understanding where you are and where you want to be in life demands that you evaluate who you are and who you want to become. To achieve your future best self, you'll need to make sacrifices, retool yourself through immersive learning experiences, and rebuild your identity. Becoming a new you requires that you learn new concepts and ideas, put your new knowledge into practice, and become an everyday learner.

## E = ENTREPRENEUR (How To Think And Act Like An Entrepreneur)

An entrepreneurial mindset is not limited to those who start their own businesses. The entrepreneur pillar of the M.U.S.C.L.E. model encourages all leaders to adopt an entrepreneurial spirit, characterized by innovation, resourcefulness, and a bias for action.

- *Ownership Mentality*: Leaders with an ownership mentality treat their teams or business units as if they were their own companies. They are deeply committed to the success of their team and take full responsibility for the outcomes. This mindset fosters accountability, initiative, and a sense of pride in one's work.

- *Resourcefulness*: Entrepreneurs are known for their ability to do more with less. They are creative problem-solvers who can find innovative ways to overcome challenges and achieve their goals. Resourceful leaders inspire their teams to be adaptable, resilient, and resourceful in the face of adversity.

If your organization is to attract and retain top talent, your leaders must be at the forefront of the battle. It's your responsibility to do two things well to attract top talent:

- Deliver training and development that helps employees learn to lead
- Motivate your employees to lead better while doing work that keeps them engaged and challenged

To find out how to build Leader M.U.S.C.L.E., keep reading.

*Dr. Bryan Deptula*
Rehoboth Beach, Delaware

# M = ME

## ALL LEADERSHIP
## STARTS WITH ME

# 1

# BELIEVE:
# LEADERS ARE BORN TO BE MADE

Without fail, no matter the audience, conference, or company, or whether working with executives or frontline employees, there was always *the one question people asked: Are leaders born or made*? The question at the genesis of why I decided to quit a six-figure salary and pursue the MBA and PhD was this: If leaders are born, and they can't be made, then what is the point of investing in leadership development and training? I had spent the better part of a decade discovering through practice and research that if you invest in people—your employees—they will work harder, smarter, more efficiently, be less likely to quit and more likely to stay, and form bonds with the company that make them care more about it and the people who lead it. For the record, return on investment (ROI) on leader development initiatives often exceeds 200 percent.[1]

Scholars have long been chipping away at the answer to the nature versus nurture question of whether leaders are born or made. The problem is that the pedantic language and complex methodologies of academic leadership research make it impossible to understand for anyone without a doctorate. As an academic, speaker, and entrepreneur, I've dedicated my career to bridging this gap between research and practice, translating rigorous research findings into actionable strategies for real-world leaders and organizations. In very real terms, I am my own audience, and I am you: a business owner who struggles with leadership every day.

## GENETIC FOUNDATIONS OF LEADERSHIP

People romanticize about *great man* theories of leadership, attributing supernatural powers to legendary historical figures[2] such as Alexander the Great and Roman Caesars. Leadership in extreme contexts such as war recalls heroes George Washington of the American Revolution, and Franklin Roosevelt and Winston Churchill during World War II. Think of civil rights champions Mahatma Gandhi of India, Nelson Mandela of South Africa, and Dr. Martin Luther King Jr. We lavish praise on J. P. Morgan, Cornelius Vanderbilt, John D. Rockefeller, and Andrew Carnegie, robber barons who built financial empires with unethical business practices, on the backs of poor laborers during the industrial and financial boom of the nineteenth century. Modern corporate empire builders are exemplified in Bill Gates, Steve Jobs, Jeff Bezos, Elon Musk, and Carlos Slim of Mexico. In popular culture, fame, fortune, glory, and power are coveted leadership outcomes. To conceptualize leaders and leadership this way is not wrong, but it is an *incomplete and contextually limited understanding* that precedes the false notion that leaders are born with special DNA and that leadership is inaccessible to common folk.

Misunderstanding who leaders are, what leadership is, where and when leadership happens, why everyone is capable of leading, and how leaders develop throughout life, blinds us from recognizing ourselves—and familiar faces of people we know—as leaders, and from recognizing leadership when it is occurring right in front of our eyes. By changing our pre-conceived and unanalyzed implicit leadership theories (there are eight distinct factors of ILTs: sensitivity, dedication, tyranny, charisma, attractiveness, masculinity, intelligence, and strength)[3, 4] we quickly recognize the humble, inglorious, selfless—with no financial reward—work of feeding impoverished people and those afflicted with leprosy, as Mother Teresa did. Leadership occurs every day, in every home and family, in our communities—educational, governmental, and religious institutions—at every level of every organization, in big and small ways.

Leaders are the parents who prepare kids for a camping trip and employees who take charge of projects or a task force. Leadership happens when teachers lead classrooms, friends organize vacations, and communities rally around a cause worth supporting. Framing leaders, leadership, and leader development in this way makes becoming a leader possible for everyone, and leadership an accessible opportunity.

The quest to understand leadership has led researchers to explore the very building blocks of human biology. At the forefront of this exploration is a series of longitudinal studies on fraternal and identical twins that sought to figure out why one twin would be in a leadership position whereas the other twin would not be.[5] These genius researchers identified a specific genetic marker associated with leadership: the rs4950 single nucleotide polymorphism on the CHRNB3 gene. This gene is involved in the production of nicotinic acetylcholine receptors, which play a crucial role in neurotransmission.

The hands-on implications of this discovery are profound: individuals with the rs4950 allele are 50 percent more likely to occupy leadership positions, suggesting a biological predisposition toward leadership behaviors. A key takeaway, though, is that only 24 percent of people expressed this rs4950 allele; meaning that select few people can attribute their leadership role to their leader genes.

A preponderance of research validates the notion that leadership genes can be inherited from ancestorial predecessors, and that age and gender influence leader emergence, with women being more likely to lead during their child-rearing years.[6]

The genetic basis of leadership is responsible for the five personality traits closely associated with effective leadership: extraversion, openness to experience, conscientiousness, emotional stability, and agreeableness. Extraversion is linked to variations in DRD4 and DRD2 genes related to dopamine transmission. Extraverts tend to be more comfortable in social situations, making them more likely to be perceived as leaders. They often exhibit higher levels of assertiveness and enthusiasm, traits that are frequently associated with effective leadership.

Openness to experience, another crucial leadership trait, is linked to variations in the KATNAL2 gene. Individuals high in openness are more receptive to new ideas and experiences. In the context of leadership, this translates to innovation and adaptability—qualities that are increasingly vital in our rapidly changing world.

Conscientiousness, associated with variations in the KATNAL2 and NMUR2 genes, manifests in individuals who tend to be organized, reliable, and goal oriented. These traits are crucial for effective leadership and task completion, often determining the difference between a vision and its successful implementation.

Emotional stability is linked to variations in the SLC6A4 gene involved in serotonin transport. Generally, higher levels of emotional stability are associated with better leadership, as these individuals tend to handle stress more effectively—a critical skill in high-pressure leadership positions. Lower levels of emotional stability lead to dysfunctional relationships, roller-coaster mood swings, and irrational outbursts that we've all been subjugated to in a toxic leader-follower relationship.

Lastly, agreeableness, associated with variations in the CLOCK gene, presents an interesting case in leadership. While high agreeableness can foster team cohesion, moderate levels are often more beneficial for leadership, allowing for the necessary assertiveness required in decision-making and direction setting.

## NEUROLOGY: A LOOK INSIDE THE LEADER'S BRAIN

The brain's neurotransmitters play a pivotal role in shaping leadership behaviors and capabilities. It's important to note that leadership involves complex cognitive and behavioral processes that can't be reduced to single neurotransmitters. These chemicals interact in intricate ways to influence behavior, mood, and cognitive function. Your genetic blueprint and neural architecture form the foundation of your leadership potential. This biological scaffolding influences everything from your decision-making style to your ability to inspire others.

Below is a nonexhaustive list of neurotransmitters that relate to leadership:

- *Dopamine*: A key neurotransmitter in the brain's reward system, influences motivation, decision-making, and risk-taking behaviors, dopamine helps leaders stay focused on goals and objectives and feel rewarded when achieving them. Leaders with optimal dopamine levels may be more decisive and action oriented, traits that can be crucial in fast-paced, high-stakes environments.

- *Serotonin*: This neurotransmitter regulates mood, social behavior, and cognitive functions, and contributes to emotional stability and interpersonal effectiveness. Balanced serotonin levels can help leaders maintain composure under pressure and navigate complex social dynamics with greater ease. Serotonin helps leaders maintain emotional stability and positive interactions with team members.

- *Endorphins*: These are the body's natural painkillers and producers of euphoria. Endorphins often can be released in response to certain rewards or achievements.

- *GABA (Gamma-Aminobutyric Acid)*: GABA aids in stress management and emotional control. It helps leaders stay calm under pressure and make rational decisions.

- *Glutamate*: Glutamate is essential for learning and memory. It enables leaders to acquire new skills, adapt to changes, and remember important information.

- *Acetylcholine*: Enhancing attention and memory, acetylcholine helps leaders stay focused during meetings and retain important details.

- *Adrenaline*: This provides the "edge" needed in high-pressure situations. It can help leaders perform well in crises or during important presentations.

- *Norepinephrine*: A neurotransmitter that increases alertness and focus, it helps leaders stay attentive during long work hours or complex problem-solving.

- *Testosterone*: Testosterone influences assertiveness and competitiveness. Moderate testosterone levels are associated with effective leadership, influencing confidence and decision-making. Conversely, excessively high levels can lead to overly aggressive authoritarian behaviors, fear-based influence tactics, and a culture of intimidation.

- *Oxytocin*: The "bonding hormone" or "trust hormone," oxytocin helps leaders build rapport, which promotes trust and social bonding. Leaders with higher oxytocin levels may be more effective in building team cohesion and fostering loyalty among their followers, creating a more unified and motivated workforce.

- *Vasopressin*: Vasopressin influences social behavior and bonding. It may play a role in a leader's ability to form strong team relationships and loyalty.

- *Cortisol*: The "stress hormone," cortisol has both positive and negative effects on leadership. In response to stress, an acute cortisol release can enhance focus and decision-making, but chronic elevated levels can impair leadership performance. When cortisol floods the body, your fight-or-flight response kicks in. Under constant stress, your brain sends signals for you to take flight and get to safety; that is to quit your job. We all know that the number one reason for turnover is that people quit their bosses. Effective leaders often show better stress management—maintaining optimal cortisol levels for peak performance without succumbing to the detrimental effects of chronic stress—and make an effort to induce appropriate amounts of stress to induce positive productivity from their workforce.

## LEADERS ARE BORN!

If you don't have the traits or gene expressions listed above, does that mean you're not going to be a leader? Of course not. And if you do have these traits and these genes, does that mean you're absolutely going to be a leader? Of course not.

Research accounts for the longitudinal "nurture" of leader development. Only by integrating findings from both nature and nurture streams of research, when observed in tandem, does a robust picture emerge of the factors that influence who will lead and how they will come to lead.

Approximately 75 to 80 percent of predictive variance of whether a person will occupy a leadership role resides in a combination of nurture and unobservable factors that influence human thinking and behaving.

Longitudinal studies of leadership development effectively delve into and explain how leaders are made through a lifespan narrative of leader identity development, exposure to leadership roles, feedback from subordinates, peers, supervisors, and biographical inputs.[7] Turns out, leaders are products of their experiences and exposure to leadership development.[8] More exposure to leadership experiences and roles leads to formation of a leader identity. Leaders claim leadership, which followers either grant or reject.[9] Life narrative research speaks mostly to how people evolve into leaders and form a leader identity throughout life, and it speaks a little of whether and how someone becomes an effective leader, and speaks less about what approach to leadership a person will take.

Perhaps the most encouraging aspect of the neuroscience of leadership is the brain's remarkable plasticity. Neuroplasticity—the brain's ability to form new neural connections—is crucial in leadership development. While genetic predispositions provide a starting point, experiences and learning can significantly alter brain structure and function.

This means that through deliberate practice and exposure to leadership experiences, individuals can enhance their leadership capabilities, regardless of their genetic starting point. It's a powerful reminder that leadership is not solely determined by our genes but is a skill that can be developed and refined over time.

## MOTIVATION TO LEAD

You can learn all day long about the traits and genes of leaders, but even in knowing what to do, how to do it, and when to do it, if you're not motivated to lead—not given the opportunity to "try" being a leader—you won't lead. Motivation to lead refers to the set of forces within a person's heart and mind, and those outside that person within the environment they're presently in; this affects the desire, intensity of effort, and a leader's (or aspiring leader's) decision to assert themselves as a leader, persist as a leader, and seek opportunities and education to develop themselves into a leader.

Research suggests people are motivated to lead by the following elements.[10] The greater the intensity of each element, the higher the person's motivation to lead (MTL):

- *Affective-Identity MTL:* This is seeing yourself as a leader. The identity of a leader isn't a separate concept because being a leader is simply "who they are." They make no distinction between the role of leader and any other part of their core identity and self-concept.

- *Emotive MTL*: Some people simply like to lead because they feel joy when leading. The more they lead, the happier they are.

- *Social-Normative MTL*: Some lead out of a sense of duty and social responsibility to help others and respect hierarchies. People with a high sense of duty and responsibility tend to have more leadership experiences.

- *Noncalculative MTL*: The willingness to lead without expecting external rewards or recognition.

A person's motivation to lead is influenced—and can be increased or decreased—by the specific work or life area in which they participate. This means people are more or less motivated to lead depending on what they're doing, who they're doing it with, and whether they want to lead in that specific context. Past leadership experiences, personality, values, and self-efficacy all influence motivation to lead. The implication of this research is the proof that factors outside of the person themself influence a person's motivation to lead. Researchers assume neither that people are motivated to lead by birth nor that a person's unconscious needs for achievement, power, or affiliation energize their motivation to lead.

The key takeaway is that—outside of all biological factors—seeing yourself as a leader, the joy of leading, and the opportunity to fulfill one's duty, as well as context and environment, are factors organizations and people can promote through training and development and organizational programs to motivate people to become leaders.

# LEADERS ARE MADE!

## WHY YOU SHOULD CARE ABOUT
## LEADER GENES AND NEUROLEADERSHIP

Understanding the genetic and neurological underpinnings of leadership has significant practical implications. I want you to stop thinking about whether leaders are born or made. Science has proven that leaders are born to be made; and that's the point of investing your time, effort, and money in leadership development and training. Yes, it is worth investing in leadership development because you can influence the emergence and performance of leaders within organizations and people in societies. Yes, for companies seeking to develop employees and for individuals seeking personal development, investing in a leadership development program has a high positive return on investment (ROI).

Think of your leader genes and neurology as foundational muscle. Some folks might have bigger muscles to start with, but anyone can build strength with the right training regimen. Ongoing leadership experiences capitalize on the brain's ability to change and adapt, allowing for continual growth and improvement in leadership capabilities.

Emerging research in neurological informed leadership reveals that our genetic makeup and brain chemistry significantly influence our leadership capabilities. By examining your leader genes and neurology, you can gain a profound understanding of your innate strengths, potential challenges, and the most effective strategies for personal and professional growth. Knowing what leader genes you do and don't have, and how your neurological programming affects your thoughts and behavior, provides a scientific basis for understanding why you might excel in certain areas of leadership naturally, and why other areas may require more effort.

This information empowers you to create a strategic personal leadership development program based on your individual genetics, neurobiology, and environmental factors that can be refined throughout your lifetime.

All the research I've studied points to this one overwhelming conclusion: At some point in their life, every person has led or will lead. If everyone will lead, that means everyone can lead. Leadership isn't some exclusive club for the genetically blessed or the corporately anointed. Leading is an innate human behavior, as natural as breathing.

Certainly, every person has had a moment in their life when they had the opportunity to be a leader. Whether they will lead, or are motivated to lead, rests on genetic, biological, and neurological factors within themselves and external factors within their environment.

# 2

## ACCELERATE YOUR
## LEADER IDENTITY AND BRAND

Legend has it that the tradition of presenting a cup to the winner(s) of sporting events has its roots in ancient Greece, where champions were awarded head wreaths and prized olive oil held within ornate golden cups. Ceremoniously, cups carry celebratory champagne for winners. Symbolically, victors can be seen envisioned to "drink in" the victory literally and metaphorically. Raising the cup in victory has a direct impact on the identity of victors; being the best at something changes your own view of yourself as well as how others view you.

Sport is an innately human activity, making its debut around fifteen thousand years ago. Cave paintings of the first forms of sport, found in Lascaux, France,[11] predate the arrival of Jesus Christ. In Christian religion, the Holy Grail is believed to be the cup that Jesus Christ drank from at the Last Supper. Joseph of Arimathea used this same cup to collect the blood of Christ as it drained from his body while hung on a crucifix. The pursuit to find the Holy Grail, a chalice, is considered one of the greatest ever endeavors of mystery and faith; driving archaeologists, King Arthur's Knights of the Round Table, and zealots alike to go on life-threatening expeditions in search of its discovery. At some point after the invention of sports and the death of Jesus Christ, humans began referring to the search for things that are extremely difficult to locate or acquire as a "quest for the Holy Grail." The saying goes that "[prestigious prize, championship, discovery] is the Holy Grail of [insert specific reference]," e.g., winning the FIFA World Cup is the Holy Grail of soccer.

The FIFA World Cup is a month-long sporting extravaganza that takes place every four years; it is indeed the Holy Grail of world soccer tournaments. The Colonial Cup, an annual winner-take-all round-robin soccer tournament, is the Holy Grail of middle school sports; to the players it feels like playing in the FIFA World Cup. I had watched winning teams heaped with praise and accolades as they raised the Colonial Cup high above their heads. My team, Gunning Bedford Middle School, had never won the tournament.

At the start of my eighth-grade season, our team got a new coach. The first words from our new coach were, "I'm a track coach who has never coached soccer, but you're stuck with me." Coach's philosophy was to use what he knew about coaching sports generally, and track specifically, and simply apply it to soccer. How different could it be, right? Wrong.

At preseason's end, Coach pulled me aside to say "Bryan, you have some skill. You're not afraid to use your voice on the field. You're going to be captain this season." *Ugh. Okay.* This was my first role as captain. I had absolutely zero leadership qualifications, and no merit to wear that captain's armband.

Laid bare was our situation: A coach who had never coached soccer. A captain who had never captained. Neither of us knowing what to do, totally making it up as we went along.

Coach announced to the team, "Every team needs a captain. Bryan is the captain of this team." Full stop. Everyone was as confused as I was. They had not known prior to that moment that "every team needs a captain," and certainly had not considered who among their peers that captain should be. Teammates had neither voted for me nor had any inclination that I was to be throned. I had not a single vote of confidence yet offered from my teammates and no mandate to fulfill on behalf of those now being captained. Rising from bended knee, several teammates offered congratulations, while others scorn, and still others not a care in the world.

It's impossible to lead without the support of those you seek to lead. When promoting people into leadership positions, leaders need to get feedback and support from followers who will be directly affected by their newly anointed "leader."

The first moment you step into a leader role is your "oh shit" moment—when you realize it's you who owns the awesome responsibility of creating the greatest good for the greatest number. And you—like everyone else—are totally unprepared.

Given your experience, knowledge, and gut instincts, you lead to the best of your abilities. You act, make decisions, and attempt to organize people in configurations to get work done, creating systems, processes, and protocols that are invariably inefficient. You fail, often, and sometimes catastrophically. If you're humble enough, you look into the mirror and acknowledge your own limitations as a human and a leader; you realize how unprepared you are to lead because you've never developed the knowledge, skills, and abilities to be a leader. You've never been trained to lead, never gained leadership experience. Few people have ever participated in any formal leadership education, training, or development. Most people don't invest the time, effort, and resources into learning to lead—and they don't teach or invest in the training and development of others.

I, like you, wasn't born knowing how to lead, who leaders

are, and what leaders really do. To figure it out, I asked: "What does the captain do, Coach?

"Do I lead the practices?

"Am I the boss?

"Should I start telling people what to do?"

Coach patted me on the head, "You'll figure it out, Bryan." He turned away without a single word of mentoring, no guidance, no books to read, neither a mention of what a captain does nor a hint of what his and the team's expectations were.

"I'm captain of the soccer team," I told my mother and my godmother MommaCis that evening.

"That's great, honey. What does that mean?" asked Mom.

"I have no idea. I wear the band during the game and tell everyone what to do, I think. I don't know. Coach didn't tell me anything except that I was captain."

Something magical happens when you get promoted, become "captain" or manager of a team—to be named *leader*. Once it happens, and you realize it is happening *to you*, there becomes within you an amazing sense of pride, strength, responsibility, and a lot of questions.

*What does it all mean...me leading people and outcomes?*

*What do leaders do?*

*Should I treat people differently?*

*What should I know about being a leader?*

*Am I any different now that I have the title than I was before being named captain?*

I had not been able to identify what had changed but knew that something about how I saw myself in relation to others had changed. This was the first time I had a responsibility for anyone other than myself. A part of who I was, and was becoming, was a leader, adding to my existing self-concept the identity of *leader*.

## LEADER IDENTITY:
## THE FOUNDATION OF EFFECTIVE LEADERSHIP

Leader identity refers to how a person sees themselves as a leader and how this self-perception influences their behavior and effectiveness in leadership roles.[12] It's not just about having a title or position; it's about internalizing the role of leader as part of who you are, as part of your self-concept. Researchers have identified four key dimensions of leader identity:[13]

- *Strength*: This refers to the degree to which a person identifies as a leader. It ranges from individuals who don't see themselves as leaders at all to those who strongly identify with the leader role. As I stood there, newly appointed as captain, my leader identity was weak. I had the title, but I didn't yet see myself as a true leader.

- *Integration*: This dimension looks at how fully the role of "leader" is woven into a person's overall self-concept. It considers how well a person sees themselves as a leader in all aspects of their life—or only in specific contexts. At this point in my journey, my leader identity was compartmentalized—I was a leader on the soccer field, but nowhere else.

- *Meaning*: This refers to a person's understanding or definition of leadership. What does it mean to be a leader? Is it about power and control, or about service and empowerment? My initial understanding of leadership was simplistic—I thought it was about being the best player and telling others what to do.

- *Inclusiveness*: This dimension considers the degree to which a leader considers others in their actions. Do you see leadership as a solo endeavor, or as a collaborative effort? In my early days as captain, I was focused on myself rather than the team, demonstrating low inclusiveness.

Developing your leader identity occurs through a process of self-reflection and growth, by aligning your actions with your values and vision of leadership. As I stood there, newly minted as captain, my leader identity was just beginning to form. I had the title, but I didn't yet have the inner conviction or understanding of what it meant to be a leader. This is a common experience for new leaders—the external recognition comes before the internal identity has fully developed.

Leaders must understand who they are as a person when they lead—they must develop a leader identity as part of their self-concept. The "self" as most people conceive of it, is a system of selves constructed from a differentiated collection of identities that define for each person "who I am." Think of your self-concept as the totality of your identities. As you enter leader roles, and have more leadership experiences, you develop part of your self-concept around the identity of leader. Identities are dynamic and complex; they are always changing based on the interpretation of new and repeated experiences in memory, evolving self- and universal-knowledge, and understanding of one's place in relationships, society, and the world at large. The mind naturally organizes each of these identities into a structure. The self exists in relation to others, such that "who I am" is structurally defined in terms of "who others are" and "who I am in relation to others."

We organize our identities in terms of how each identity represents "who we are" in various roles. Immediately after birth, humans begin constructing identities around each role they play; the most basic among them being son/daughter, brother/sister, and leader/follower. Society reinforces the two roles of leader and follower with children's games such as "follow the leader." As we "play" various roles, our mind begins to assign diverse attributes to the role being enacted in each moment.

Self-aspects are personal attributes that influence behavior and performance in each role. Only limited aspects of the self are prompted by the current situations or experiences, which then activates one identity from the collection of possible identities, what is known as "the working self-concept." The mind scans the environment and then prioritizes which identity is most relevant in the moment; and then it activates that identity as the working self-concept. At any given moment, the person who you "are" is really the working self-concept that has been brought forward for the period that identity is relevant and necessary. Whatever is the role we are presently engaged in will determine the identity we call forward in that moment. Think about your working self-concept at work and how different that is from the identity in use when you kiss your children goodnight, or play sports, or engage in religious or spiritual activities. In this way, people distinguish which "self" is relevant in a particular circumstance.

Every person forms, transforms, and modifies how they define themselves; based on, among other things, their life experiences, achievements, social status, education, working knowledge of how they see themselves in relation to others, and their responses and reactions to situations and activities.[14]

## LEADER BRAND: YOUR LEADERSHIP SIGNATURE

While leader identity is about how you see yourself as a leader, leader brand is about how others perceive you as a leader. It's the unique combination of qualities, values, behaviors, and achievements that define you as a leader in the eyes of others. Think of it as your leadership signature—the distinctive mark you leave on the people who observe you—your team, organization, and industry.[15]

A strong leader brand can open doors, attract opportunities, and inspire loyalty in your team. It's what sets you apart in a crowded marketplace of leaders. In the postpandemic world, where personal interactions are often limited to virtual spaces, your leader brand is more important than ever. It's what people see and experience of you online, in meetings, and through your communication. It's what shapes their perception of your leadership abilities.

A strong leader brand is built on authenticity, consistency, and a clear value proposition. It's about communicating your vision, values, and expertise in a way that resonates with your audience. It's about building trust and credibility through your actions and interactions.

Surely, my caretakers had instilled confidence in me, and encouraged me to believe in myself. That is the job of parents, caretakers, and "transformational leaders": to make you believe in yourself, that you can achieve anything you set your mind to, that you can perform beyond your own expectations, and that you can take ownership of your own outcomes.[16]

My godmother, who came to every practice and game I ever had, knew that being captain meant that I had to grow as a person. As my leader, she took her responsibility to develop me into a leader very seriously. MommaCis gave me the gentle guidance to begin developing my leader identity.

"Bryan, *you* are the *leader*. Being captain means that other members of the team look to *you* for leadership. This is an honor, to be selected as captain. You must seize the opportunity to learn, to lead, and to be the very best captain that you can be. Captains are leaders, and with that role comes the responsibility of helping your teammates form into a team.

"You need to figure out who you want to be in the leader role: a person with a responsibility to take care of the people you lead, harnessing the potential of collaborative power with relationships. Or will you be a person who uses their power over others for personal benefit?

"You must *see yourself* as a leader, and your teammates must also see that you are their leader. You must *be* the example on the field of how to play the game. Teammates, teachers, principals, and administrators are looking for leadership off the field as well. Leaders set the example of the behaviors they want to see in others—when they operate under the 'do as I do' rule. Approach your teammates differently, more positively. Play with greater vigor than ever before. Coach and your teammates are counting on you."

MommaCis pushed me to realize the magnitude of being a leader. Slowly, steadily, all these messages started to sink into my brain. I started to see how my behavior, the things I was saying, my work ethic, the way I treated others, all served as an indicator to my teammates about appropriate behavior.

I began to "claim" leader roles,[17] which furthered the development of my leader identity. Claiming an identity occurs when you assert yourself as either a leader or follower. My natural extroversion made others "see" me as a leader, causing them to "grant" me the roles to which I aspired. Granting a leader identity to another person reinforces and strengthens a given identity, while rejection challenges identity. With every instance of claiming and granting, I developed knowledge to flex my leader identity and brand muscles.

Claiming and granting experiences add to your development of a leader identity. Every episode where I laid claim to—and was granted—leader roles contributed to my emerging leader identity. An accurate understanding of the self is drawn by reflecting on the total set of experiences we have leading others—in any capacity and role.

## THE UNKNOWN UNKNOWN

The regular season passed and with it came the "Colonial Cup." We made it to the finals, something our team had never achieved before. The championship game was tied 0-0 at the end of regulation time and overtime, leading to a penalty shoot-out.

As the referees explained the shoot-out rules to Coach, his face contorted from dazed and confused into panic; he had no prior experience with—and limited if any working knowledge of—soccer itself, the rules of the tournament, strategy for penalty shoot-outs, and a great many other nuanced elements of the sport. This was a classic example of an "unknown unknown"—something a person should have known about but doesn't realize they need to know. The unknown unknown is a blind spot, ignorance of what the thing is conceptually. In short, the person doesn't know what they don't know. Coaching and leading by simply "what you know" is just *not* good enough.

Unfortunately, the unknown unknown for Coach was the penalty shoot-out. This being his first time encountering the penalty phase of a contest, he was wholly unprepared to lead. Worse, he allowed his team to enter a dramatic sports climax entirely unrehearsed. Coach had not thought to prepare us for the contingency of a penalty shoot-out because he had not developed the proper knowledge of the game to foresee a highly predictable eventuality.

The shoot-out began. Our first shooter scored, but so did theirs. Our second shooter missed, while theirs scored. Our third shooter missed again, and theirs scored. By the time our fourth shooter approached the ball, we were down 1-3. The pressure was overwhelming, and he missed. We had lost before I, as the fifth shooter, even got a chance to take my shot.

This experience taught me a harsh truth: A leader's identity, how they see themselves, directly affects their behaviors. Coach's leader identity was a "know-it-all," as he internalized an image of himself of being able to wing it better than anyone else. His brand: a cavalier hotshot. Thus, because he saw himself as a "lead-on-the-fly" type of coach, he willfully and intentionally chose not to prepare himself by learning the rules of the game. This toxic combination bred a dangerous overconfidence, stifling any inclination to learn or prepare adequately for his role. His unwavering belief in his own infallibility blinded him to his glaring knowledge gaps, leaving him woefully ill-equipped to lead effectively when anything extraordinary (like a penalty shoot-out) changes the game. The huge gap between his perceived and actual competence set the stage for inevitable failure.

A leader's failure to prepare has devastating consequences for their team; a leader's lack of preparation leads to their followers/teams/companies being unprepared to succeed. When a leader lacks knowledge or expertise in their field, they lack the ability to think critically and anticipate potential eventualities that will determine outcomes, are more likely to make poor decisions, miss opportunities, and ultimately fail to achieve their goals.

Being blindsided by an unknown unknown is often avoidable through preparation. When assuming a leadership role, it's crucial to become knowledgeable about the role itself, the context in which it's performed, and specific job-related knowledge. This preparation helps leaders provide expert-level feedback and direction. The pandemic exposed how being unprepared for what's coming next can severely limit a leader's perspective and effectiveness.

The COVID-19 pandemic served as a stark reminder of the impact of "unknown unknowns" on leadership. Despite being a highly predictable eventuality, with numerous warnings from health experts and pandemic simulations, it caught most leaders off guard. This global crisis exposed a critical lack of preparation among leaders across various sectors, challenging their ability to respond effectively to unprecedented circumstances.

The pandemic, like the soccer tournament for my coach, exposed numerous unknown unknowns for organizational leaders. Many made the critical error of assuming their pre-existing knowledge and experiences would seamlessly translate to the new context. While some universal leadership principles remained applicable—such as building trust and motivating employees—completely different working conditions, the integration of new technology, and constantly changing state and federal regulations demanded new approaches.

Leaders discovered that while some of their experience could be applied in commonsense ways to the new situation, much of what they knew about leading in a prepandemic world was insufficient or even counterproductive. The gap between what leaders knew and what they needed to know to navigate the pandemic environment often led to significant business challenges.

## LEADER IDENTITY AND BRAND
## IN A POSTPANDEMIC WORLD

Leader identity and brand are dynamic concepts that must evolve with changing circumstances. The pandemic starkly illustrated this reality. Just as my middle school soccer coach clung to his track coaching methods, many leaders stubbornly adhered to prepandemic leadership styles, rendering themselves ineffective. Others and I astutely observed that everything in the world had shifted, and intentionally reevaluated who we were then and who we had to become in order to lead now. We recognized that effective leadership in a hybrid world demanded more than just acquiring new skills; it required a fundamental shift in self-perception (identity) and desired public image (brand).

I declare that the leadership failures and struggles we saw during the pandemic resulted from leaders having an identity crisis. The pandemic served as a great equalizer, exposing the same fatal flaws in leaders across industries and nations. Like Coach, many executives had cultivated identities as infallible visionaries and brands of unwavering confidence, leaving them blindsided when confronted with an unprecedented crisis. Their perceived omniscience crumbled in the face of a virus that respected neither hierarchy nor hubris. Suddenly, the bravado that had once been their hallmark became a liability, as the new workforce demanded their bosses be more empathetic to their needs and sensitive to new working conditions where everyone was literally isolated. The pandemic mercilessly revealed the gulf between their inflated self-perception and the harsh reality of their limitations, forcing a reckoning with their own inadequacies. The abrupt transition to remote work meant that leaders had to learn to inspire and motivate through screens, requiring a fundamental change in communication style and a deeper understanding of virtual team dynamics. Many who had built their leadership personas on face-to-face charisma and micromanagement found themselves struggling to adapt to virtual environments. This internal identity crisis directly affected both their willingness to learn new skills and ability to lead the postpandemic workforce.

Those who failed to prepare for this change saw their brand perception shift negatively. The inability to adapt to digital leadership not only hampered team productivity but also damaged leaders' reputations and effectiveness. Leaders who clung to outdated self-perceptions and practices often faltered, while those who embraced the need for identity evolution thrived.

The pandemic forced a profound transformation in my leadership approach and self-perception. I had to rapidly adapt from relying on in-person charisma to engaging effectively across various platforms, including socially distanced sessions and digital meetings. This shift wasn't just about changing mediums; it fundamentally challenged and reshaped how I saw myself—and how others saw me—as a speaker and trainer.

As I learned to connect through screens and maintain engagement without physical presence, I developed new skills and perspectives. My leader identity evolved from being primarily a dynamic in-person presenter to a versatile, tech-savvy communicator who inspired audiences across multiple formats. This transformation affected how others perceived me.

There has never been a time in history where having strong leadership fundamentals and being able to quickly adapt one's leadership to evolving contexts has been as important as during the pandemic. Just as our coach needed to adapt his track-based coaching style to soccer, leaders during the pandemic had to adapt their prepandemic leadership styles to a new, virtual world. This meant developing new skills like virtual team management, digital communication, and remote performance evaluation. Preexisting leadership skills were necessary but not sufficient for the new challenges. Typically, leaders faced three challenges:

- *Anchoring Bias*: Leaders often clung to prepandemic practices due to anchoring bias, a cognitive tendency that resists change even when it's necessary. The mindset of "I am who I am, and it's gotten me this far" exemplifies an inflexible, nonadaptive identity. For instance, leaders accustomed to hierarchical management struggled to adapt to the decentralized, team-based approach better suited for remote work. Their reluctance to empower employees and delegate decision-making hindered innovation and agility. This inflexibility can be partially explained by the interplay of neurotransmitters:

  - Cortisol: The pandemic induced chronic stress, leading to constant cortisol release. This state inhibits learning and causes reliance on familiar patterns.

  - Glutamate (aids learning and memory): Under normal conditions, open-minded leaders would experience glutamate release, facilitating the development of new leadership skills. The pandemic's prolonged stress disrupted this balance, making it harder for leaders to adapt to the unprecedented societal and workplace changes.

- *Lack Of Digital Fluency*: The shift to remote work exposed a critical gap in many leaders' digital literacy. Essential skills like using videoconferencing platforms to create a sense of presence, conducting online performance reviews that focus on results rather than micromanaging, and fostering virtual team building through online games and social activities were unfamiliar territory for many. This lack of fluency made it difficult for them to build trust and rapport with their teams in a virtual environment and generated feelings of isolation and disconnection among team members. Leaders who didn't learn to communicate saw their brands diminished, as people saw them as lacking the skills and experience necessary to manage and motivate virtual teams effectively.

- *Underinvestment In Training And Development*: Many organizations, caught off guard by the pandemic, failed to invest in leadership development programs that could have equipped their leaders with the skills needed to navigate the challenges of the new world of work. These programs could have addressed areas such as digital communication, providing effective feedback in a virtual environment, building resilience in a crisis, and fostering a culture of psychological safety where employees feel comfortable speaking up with concerns or ideas. As a result, many leaders felt overwhelmed and unprepared, leading to a decline in employee engagement, and increased stress levels. Their brand value declined as followers observed their inability to lead during crisis and inability to level up their skills to meet the challenges.

The challenges posed by the pandemic highlighted a crucial aspect of leadership: adaptability. Leaders who successfully navigated the crisis demonstrated their capacity for change, not only to their teams but also to themselves. This adaptability becomes a defining characteristic of their leadership identity and enhanced the perceived value they add as a leader.

Internally, leaders who embraced adaptability during the pandemic experienced a shift in self-perception. They came to see themselves as capable of handling unexpected challenges and pivoting their strategies when necessary. Externally, these leaders developed a brand reputation for being prepared and adaptable, no matter the situation. Their ability to navigate the pandemic's complexities became a hallmark of their leadership brand, earning them the trust and respect of their teams and peers.

## LESSONS IN HUMILITY AND IDENTITY CONSTRUCTION

My own life was changed in the very moment that I did not get to take that penalty shot. I knew failure intimately from then on: mine and my coach's. It was the first time in my life where I recognized my importance as a leader and my responsibility to know how to lead. Although I believed myself to have some influence on my teammates, I was never named captain of a sport team again. These experiences of humility and setback were crucial in shaping my leader identity. They taught me that leadership isn't about being the best performer, but about bringing out the best in others.

The pandemic also forced many of us to confront our own limitations and vulnerabilities. Just as I had to come to terms with not being the star athlete I thought I was, many leaders had to acknowledge that they didn't have all the answers in the face of an unprecedented global crisis. This humility, when coupled with a commitment to learn and adapt, often led to more authentic and effective leadership.

I did not win the Colonial Cup. My goal now is to develop leaders around the world, most importantly my children, into bold and humble leaders that more often than me succeed in taking their shot.

# 3

# **LEAD YOURSELF FIRST**

Every Saturday MommaCis would knock on my door at the crack of dawn to say, "Time to clean your room and do your laundry."

For the most part, my room was always clean. Each day I would make my bed. Three reasons compelled me to tidy up those sheets every morning and clean them weekly. First is that I have always been, and still am, accomplishment driven. Making my bed before I left the house gave me the comfort of knowing that I could go about my day having started by accomplishing this very small task.

The second reason was that I spent most of my time in my room. When I spend time in a place, I want that place to be clean. Making your bed is a good place to start cleaning.

The third reason was practical: I would clean my sheets because they would be filthy from a week's worth of mud, dirt, and perspiration from a sweaty pubescent boy with raging hormones. Going to bed without a shower happened a lot. By the end of each week, my room smelled like the bottom of a gym locker; sheets would almost be yellow and brown. My teenage body odor could be described in one word: funky.

Laundry was another concern. For as long as I can remember, I've done my own laundry—with a little help from Mom and MommaCis. Maybe it's because I started sorting my own laundry at such a young age that I never bought into the universally accepted method for sorting laundry: lights and whites in one pile, darks and colors in another pile. I had two piles of clothes, and I sorted them according to how fast I could get them done: dirty and funky. MommaCis would look at my piles with a sad and confused face, as though she had failed me as a parent. "Why do you do it that way? I know doing laundry isn't fun, but you always get it done," MommaCis said.

As I explained to MommaCis, "Since I must, I'd like to spend as little time as possible performing this miserable task. I would rather do anything else but laundry. I take no pleasure in the act of laundry-ing. Since it is my responsibility, and I don't want to go to school looking like a hobo, I got no choice. I take gently used items and put them in the fast cycle, basically a rinse and spin. The funky pile takes a full wash plus some extra loving to make sure the clothes get clean. I take any measure I can to shorten the time between laundry washing and drying and folding. Plus, I think your system of lights and whites, colors and darks is broken; at least it doesn't work for me. So, I made my own system. More efficient my way."

"Humph," she would snort and walk away.

This simple act of completing not-fun-but-necessary tasks such as making my bed and doing my own laundry were, unknown to me at the time, my first step into self-leadership. Self-leadership begins with small, consistent actions that build over time into larger patterns of behavior.[18]

Reflection question: Think about your daily routines. What small actions do you take that might be building your self-leadership muscles without you even realizing it?

## SELF-LEADERSHIP

By definition, "self-leadership is a process through which people influence themselves to achieve the self-direction and self-motivation necessary to behave and perform in desirable ways."[19] To lead yourself is to be able to self-influence, which requires self-regulation, self-control, and self-management. Self-leadership involves specific sets of behavioral and cognitive strategies that give rise to the outcomes a person may create for themselves. Three broad strategic categories encompass self-leadership: (a) behavior-focused strategies, (b) natural reward-based strategies, and (c) constructive thought/pattern strategies.

## BEHAVIOR-FOCUSED STRATEGIES IN ACTION

The purpose of behavior-focused strategies is to increase self-awareness, so that you can manage behaviors that lead to the accomplishment of necessary but unpleasant tasks. Give yourself positive encouragement that creates desirable behaviors and leads to successful outcomes, while suppressing negative, undesirable behaviors. Behavior-focused strategies foster self-discipline, increase personal effectiveness, and create positive habits that lead to long-term success and well-being. In my case, I had set a goal to efficiently manage my laundry. I observed that the traditional sorting method wasn't working for me, so I self-corrected by creating my own system.

Proactively leading yourself involves five processes:

- *Self-Observation*: Heighten your awareness of when and why you engage in specific behaviors; be mindful of your own actions, thoughts, and patterns.

- *Self-Goal Setting*: Establish specific, challenging, and achievable goals for yourself that align with your broader objectives and values.

- *Self-Reward*: Treat yourself to valued rewards (tangible or intangible) when you accomplish goals or important tasks.

- *Self-Punishment*: In the positive, you give yourself self-correcting feedback to induce a change in behavior. In the negative, you give yourself unconstructive self-criticism or guilt when failing to meet goals or engaging in undesirable behaviors.

- *Self-Cueing*: Create reminders and cues to keep yourself on track, which you place throughout all your environments, including to-do lists, sticky notes, and digital reminders.

## NATURAL REWARD STRATEGIES: FINDING JOY IN THE MUNDANE

Natural reward strategies focus on creating or emphasizing enjoyable aspects of activities to enhance intrinsic motivation (that is, the self-induced motivation); they create a sense within yourself of competence, self-control, and purpose. The goal is to generate positive feelings that naturally result from performing the activity itself, rather than relying solely on external rewards; this leads to improved performance, greater job satisfaction, and reduced feelings of need for external motivators such as pay and promotion.

Natural reward strategies involve two primary approaches:[20]

- *Building Pleasant And Rewarding Features Into Activities*: Restructure tasks or the work environment to make them more enjoyable or change your perception of the task to make it more inherently enjoyable.

- *Shaping Perceptions By Focusing Attention On Rewarding Aspects*: Highlight the pleasurable parts of tasks and activities. I never delighted in the activity of doing laundry. Rather, the satisfaction of accomplishing a task was satisfying. And I have never been above doing any type of work, especially when that dirty work was of my own making. By focusing on the satisfaction of task completion rather than the task itself, I was unknowingly employing natural reward strategies.

Breaking inefficient systems and reinventing new and more efficient workflows and procedures is one of my favorite things to do. Perhaps this habit of mine started with laundry. Whenever there is a system that I don't like, at home or in an office, on a team or on my own, I will break it and then reimagine all the moving bits and pieces into a value-maximizing new arrangement. A truism that always holds, regardless of context: When you put the best person against the worst system, try as that person might, the system will almost always win. So, in my eternal pursuit of self-leadership, I break stuff all the time, always striving for the natural reward of discovering a better way. This desirable characteristic is what makes me an excellent consultant—that I can identify broken systems and reimagine them in creative and innovative ways to capture efficiencies and increase productivity.

I don't like this expression: If it isn't broke don't fix it. To me, if we accept that the system works, we accept that it is optimized, and systems are rarely optimized, because we humans too often unquestioningly accept things as they are and don't challenge the universally accepted standard way of doing a thing. My question was/is: What if the way the system/thing was designed was inefficient from the beginning? What then, are we supposed to keep on being inefficient and under-productive simply because the system works? If it isn't broke and doesn't need fixing, then certainly it is good to constantly reexamine the system for fine tuning and opportunities to tweak it into higher efficiency and better use of resources.

Now, as an adult leader, I encourage my followers to break things all the time. Instead of fighting the system, I have always found it a more profitable use of my time and intellect to change the system. Plus, once the system is changed, more people can work more efficiently, are happier that they don't have to fight a system that doesn't work and are more productive. In my case, I used my laundry time more efficiently, was happier not to have to color-code my laundry piles, and had more time for fun, sports, and studying. Fortunately, neither Mom nor MommaCis forced me to accept conventional wisdom, and I was free to explore this habit of breaking things under the encouragement of flexible caretakers who only cared that I "got it done." To me, the only system that I am committed to is the one that is ruthlessly efficient, maximizes my—and my family's and followers—time and productivity.

MommaCis knew my method of sorting laundry would be put to the test when I moved into my first apartment. She drove me to almost every sports practice and game I ever had, for my entire life. During these road trips together she and I would reveal my darkest secrets, pose questions about life, and pontificate on the meaning of things I didn't understand. She would ask me questions about my life, and we would sort through the world's problems. There was never a time that we weren't engaged in conversations—all manner of discussion, sometimes laughing and other times me intently listening to life lessons she doled out. She was my trusted confidant, my sounding board. There wasn't a thing in the world that I hid from her. Our safe space made it permissible to be truthful about my feelings and inner workings. Once I was in my own apartment, our alone time in the car vanished, and with it the space for us to enjoy one another's company.

She recognized an opportunity to recapture time between us, savvy ole bird that she was. "Bring your laundry home every weekend. I'll do it for you. Put some food in your belly while you wait for it to be done. No dropping it off though. Laundry can be done only while you're here," she said. Laundry takes two hours minimum for two loads. In the window of time it took to wash and fold my laundry, we would share time together. Every weekend I would show up with a full bag of dirty duds. Smiling, both of us knew that I could do my own laundry; both of us took comfort knowing that bringing my laundry was the new and efficient system we had designed to both accomplish a task and be in one another's presence. On my departures, my bags were full of clean clothes and our hearts were full of love.

## LEADING MYSELF THROUGH DEATH

Ring. Ring. The phone called out.

"Hello."

My mom was on the other end of the phone: "MommaCis. Bryan. MommaCis..."

"What? You're not speaking in complete sentences. What's going on?" I knew, though, what was going on. I could feel it, sense it in my core. MommaCis was dead.

"Your sister found her slumped over onto the kitchen table. Go directly to the ER entrance," Mom said.

Laundry went flying everywhere. As fast as my POS car would move, I raced to the hospital and into the ER. There was no reason for my speeding or sprinting. She was already gone. My godmother. Dead. Heart attack. Her warm dead body lay on the ambulance bed she had been placed on to remove her body from our home.

I cried. She did not shed a tear.

I held her hand. She did not hold mine back.

I asked, *Why have you left me?* She made no reply.

*Who is going to do my laundry?*

*Who am I going to talk to?*

*I am not ready for you to be gone.*

There is nothing in the world that can prepare a person for the loss of their caretaker, their most intimate lifelong relation-ship, the most important person in their world, the one who was responsible for feeding them, clothing them, keeping them alive.

I was devastated, lost, less whole, less alive. A part of me died when MommaCis passed away. There was less of me, less life, less happiness, and more sadness and confusion.

In the hazy images that played out in front of me were mouths moving with sounds coming out that fell on my deaf ears.

Shock set in.

Muttering under my breath. Walking in circles, staring at the circles my feet traced.

Barely into my junior year of college, not even twenty-one years of age, and my entire universe had been ripped out from me. Mercilessly. Death. MommaCis's passing left me with only my mom, sister, and godfather as family, and only a couple friends who I grew up with. Few people from my childhood remained, and their surviving families living but my connections to them dead.

I cried on the way home from the hospital. I cried morning, noon, and night every day until MommaCis's funeral. I cried on the way to the church service. I cried during the priest's oration and all the way to the cemetery. I cried walking to my VIP front-row seat at the funeral. I cried the whole way through the reading and during the last words ever to grace her body before she was interred into the ground.

Sitting there on that fake grass that outlined the eight feet of dug up earth that would become MommaCis's final resting place, I watched the casket lower slowly until the rope ran its full length and the wheels stopped, indicating her descent was final. Mourners slowly disbanded into cars that left the graveyard until no one but she and I were left.

It had been my experience that funeral receptions were always sad affairs: everyone standing around crying and sniffling, making false promises to stay in touch. Mom hosted the reception at her house. All mourners were socializing, hugging, and the oddest thing, laughing.

MommaCis was a hard-drinking, fun-loving, tough-as-nails, softball-playing, fist-fighting, soft-on-the-inside-and-hard-on-the-outside Irish lesbian. Everyone at the funeral reception matched her description, save that not all of them were Irish. Each of those ladies had known me since before I had come out of diapers. They had seen me grow up and been a part of my life. I loved every one of those ladies standing there as though they were at a birthday party. No one offered me condolences. There was not one platitude of "she's in a better place." These ladies raised their cups full of whiskey into the air, and gave me a high five and a hug, or a pat on the arse with a wink. There was no sadness, only celebration. A celebration of life, on MommaCis's burial day.

"Remember the time when MommaCis hurled an ice ball at those thugs," said one softball teammate. "Charlotte Murphy didn't take shit from nobody."

"Oh, the stories about your godmother. She was the funniest lady in the world. There wasn't a time when she wasn't pulling a prank on someone in the dugout," said another.

"Boy, your MommaCis loved you. Growing up, you were always on her lap; or as a toddler standing behind her back as she drove into the parking lot. And then you got big enough, so we had to come watch your ball games. Much love from your godmother. I remember things about you that you probably don't remember about yourself. Let's have a drink together. You're old enough now, and it's about time that we start celebrating proper," said another "Aunt."

This wasn't like any funeral reception I had ever been to. Everyone knew better than to send MommaCis off with tears, for fear that she might come back to haunt them. In death, she was as big a figure as she was in life. They were taking time to recall all the good things about her and the life that she lived. Whiskey and memories flowed. Great food and even better stories were shared. No one was leaving. We were over five hours into the party when a torrential rain poured down.

A few of my friends came to the funeral and the reception. Blaze, Paxton, and I climbed on top of the shed in the backyard. Rain poured on us. Sitting there on that shed rooftop, we laughed and cried. MommaCis was part of their lives too; she treated them as her sons.

"You ever wonder if the dead can hear us? If they are with us? If they can see us?" asked Blaze.

"Don't know brother," said Paxton, "it would be great if MommaCis saw us celebrating her life."

"You think she's watching?" asked Blaze.

"Only one way to find out boys. Let's ask her." That said, I looked up into the heavens, deep into the eye of the storm, and shouted at the top of my lungs, "MommaCis. If you are up there in heaven, looking down, give us a sign. Any sign. Just let us know that you'll be here with us. That you see how much we love you."

Crack. A flash of lightening.

We three looked at each other. *Did that just happen?*

In all the time since that rainstorm had started there had not been a single clap of thunder or bolt of lightning—not one sound except for pouring rain hitting the rooftop.

"MommaCis, is that you? Send us a sign. Talk to us."

Boom. Thunder clapped.

Flash. Lightning lit up the sky.

"I love you MommaCis. I know that you are here with us."

"She's here. We love you," shouted Paxton and Blaze.

The next morning, I woke up with two friends on the floor next to me. Sadness was gone. My heart opened with love, knowing that MommaCis was with me in spirit. These were not the feelings that I had had from previous deaths. I had grown accustomed to being swallowed by anger or confusion, darkness and sadness, but I felt none of those feelings.

The only things I felt were gratitude for the time God gave me with MommaCis, happiness that she was the biggest part of my life, thankfulness that she raised me to be a respectful man, and comfort from the love that her memory offered. I felt more whole, more complete, full of love.

I closed my eyes and laid back down. Her presence sat next to me in the chair where she had sat so many times before. Her voice called to me, "I am not gone. Who will you become? I have given you the tools to be a great man. Will you be the man I taught you to be?" I turned to my right and talked to her as if her physical body were there. This was our final ride together: her to a tomb of eternal life beyond earth and me to a new path of grieving. I talked to her. I let her know that I would miss her and that I loved her. Although we wouldn't be in person taking our rides together, we would certainly now spend more time together, seeing as how her spirit could spend time with me any place or anytime she wanted. I told her I'd be a gentleman, courteous to everyone, always tell the truth, and make her proud. Truth be told, she was a better listener now than ever.

When loved ones had previously passed away, I suffered under the stress of their loss; I engaged in dysfunctional thought processes. I suppressed all the pain, and I buried all my emotions down deep with the memories of their existence. There was no grieving, no grief therapy, no healing. Just chaos. I became convinced that my time on earth was close to an end, and I operated under the assumption that sooner rather than later God would punch my ticket. Now, though, we had reinvented the process of grieving. We reimagined all the bits and pieces of sadness and transformed them into a celebration, a much more efficient and productive way to process the loss of a loved one. We had accomplished a wonderful task: joining together in heart-ache to come out together as one whole body that celebrated the life of MommaCis.

Now, though, from the great dugout beyond, MommaCis encouraged me to think constructively. I imagined myself being happy despite her loss and placed myself in scenes where her feedback was put to good use to spawn a bright happy future.

## CONSTRUCTIVE THOUGHT STRATEGIES

The final component of self-leadership consists of constructive thought strategies: strategies that include the creation and continuance of purposeful patterns of habitual thinking that improve performance.[21] Thinking constructively involves evaluating and challenging your own irrational beliefs and assumptions, painting positive mental imagery of your performing with success, and engaging in positive self-talk.

Constructive thought strategies include:[22]

- *Self-Analysis And Improvement Of Belief Systems*: Examine and alter dysfunctional beliefs and assumptions; challenge and replace self-defeating thoughts with constructive ones.

- *Positive Self-Talk*: Use positive internal dialogues or self-statements to influence one's behavior and performance.

- *Mental Imagery*: Visualize successful performance of a task before it is completed.

- *Opportunity Thinking*: Reframe obstacles as opportunities for growth or innovation.

- *Rational Self-Analysis*: Logically examine and manage negative or irrational internal dialogues.

Through a process of self-analysis, I began self-dialogue. *Death is as much a part of life as birth. Loss is not the opposite of gain, because you never truly lose the ones who you loved while they lived.* By engaging in positive self-talk, I was breaking my own dysfunctional psychological and emotional processes of dealing with death. *Their life is to be celebrated, remembered, and cherished. All the moments they spent with you are departing gifts that your deceased family and friends gave to you when they left the mortal world.*

Then, I gave myself the encouragement to be strong, to break the cycle of going down the black hole of emotional despair that accompanied all the previous deaths. It was a sad fact of life that I was so familiar with death, and the destructive pattern needed a death of its own. *Death is not your enemy. Death gives you beginnings to new chapters in life. Live on young man. Live life like you just got shot out of a rocket, live on its edges, to its absolute maximum. Live not in fear of death but in fulfillment of your purpose. MommaCis is gone, but you still have her voice in your head, the memories you created, the moral compass she embedded in your being, and the rules for being a good and decent human being. Most importantly, self, she gave you wisdom to know when you need to change direction in life, and the confidence to pivot away from bad and toward good with all your energy—no matter how risky or scary change might be, figure out your path and pivot fearlessly.*

Instead of playing the "woe-is-me" card, I became even

more motivated to cram as much into life as possible. I made more friends without fear of losing them. I smiled more and enjoyed life's little moments more. I took the time to extend small kindnesses to others. I softened my heart to the pain of others. I made myself available to the full range of positive and negative emotions. I was resolute in my love of life. I challenged grief, and led myself to victory, and rewarded myself healthfully when accomplishing milestones that MommaCis would have been proud of.

I took death and I broke it. I was sick and tired of being sick and tired of people dying around me. I was going to live, damn it, and live the best life I could. I found a way to sort through two piles of life experiences: light and bright, and *funky*. Certainly, I acknowledged death; but I was now able to navigate troubled waters with the experience of an experienced seaworthy captain. From MommaCis's death onwards, most of my time was spent seeking the light and bright experiences. I changed the process and reinvented how I chose to experience the bits and pieces of life to effectively lead myself. MommaCis's death, it turned out, invigorated me to live.

I had a choice. You have a choice. Choose life. Choose to lead yourself. Lead yourself, first; for if you cannot lead yourself, you are not prepared to lead anyone else.

That's the way she would have wanted it: me...*livin'*! *Leading*! And that's the way I want it for you.

## WHY YOU SHOULD CARE ABOUT SELF-LEADERSHIP

You might be thinking, "Why should I care about self-leadership? I'm already successful. I get things done." Know this: Being productive and being a leader are very different things.

Anyone can follow orders and complete tasks, but true leadership comes from within. It's about self-awareness, self-determination, self-regulation, and self-motivation. Self-leadership isn't just about personal growth—leading yourself is the single most important thing you can do to effectively lead others.

## YOU MUST FIRST LEARN TO LEAD YOURSELF BEFORE YOU CAN ATTEMPT TO LEAD OTHERS

Self-leadership is about consciously directing your thoughts, behaviors, and motivations to achieve your goals and maximize your potential; making conscious effort requires persistence and self-awareness.

Look in the mirror and you'll see a reflection of yourself. That reflection is what other people see and imitate. The human brain is filled with "mirror neurons"—brain cells that fire both when we perform an action and when we observe someone else performing the same action. Our brains are wired to mimic the behavior of those around us. This is why we yawn when we see someone else yawn, or why we smile when we see someone else smile. Mirror neurons are the basis for learning, empathy, and social behavior.[23]

The field of Neuroleadership emphasizes the importance of understanding brain function in leadership development. The SCARF model, for instance, outlines five domains of social experience that activate either the "primary reward" or "primary threat" circuitry of the brain: status, certainty, autonomy, relatedness, and fairness. By practicing self-leadership and modeling positive behaviors, giving yourself natural rewards and thinking constructively, you create a brain-friendly environment that promotes engagement and performance.[24]

Leading yourself changes your own neural pathways and behaviors and positively reshapes your influence on others—as they see you lead yourself, others are inclined to mirror your positive behaviors and improve their own lives and leadership. The positive benefits and power of self-leadership can transform your family, the individuals you lead, the teams you manage, your entire organization, and your community.

Think about your daily opportunities for self-leadership: setting and pursuing goals, managing your emotional responses, maintaining focus in the face of distractions. Each of these actions not only improves your own performance but also sets a neural pattern for those around you to follow: your team unconsciously imitates your behavior, attitude, and approach to challenges. As a leader who now understands the influence of mirror neurons on directing followers' behaviors, you should proactively use your self-leadership as an unstated directive that demonstrates what you value, how you get work done, and the behaviors you want to see in followers. When you demonstrate strong self-leadership, you're creating a neural template for your team to follow. Effective leaders activate neural networks associated with positive emotions and social engagement in their followers, leading to increased motivation, creativity, and overall performance.[25]

When, because you lead yourself well, you are calm, confident, and in control of your emotions, your team will mirror those behaviors. Individuals who practice effective self-leadership often experience positive emotions, which can correlate with higher serotonin levels. You can literally induce a physiological change in your followers' serotonin levels. Your calmness becomes their calmness. Your confidence becomes their confidence. Reward centers in both your and their brains are activated, releasing neurotransmitters like dopamine that reinforce positive habits and drive continued growth and achievement. When you're leading yourself, you enjoy the benefits of norepinephrine, which increases your alertness and focus, helping you—and them—work through complex problems.

Conversely, when you are not actively practicing self-leadership—not setting goals, maintaining discipline, engaging in positive self-talk—you are setting a neural example that self-leadership is neither necessary nor valuable. Your team's mirror neurons will pick up on your lack of self-discipline and goal setting and your negative self-talk, and they will unconsciously replicate these patterns. When, because you fail to lead yourself, you are constantly stressed, overwhelmed, and lacking self-care, guess what? Your stress becomes their stress. Your overwhelm becomes their overwhelm. Both your and their brains release cortisol, causing a mental and physiological shut down in thinking and acting.

GABA is an inhibitory neurotransmitter, meaning it helps calm the nervous system. When stress levels rise, the body's stress response system is activated, leading to an increase in excitatory neurotransmitters like adrenaline and cortisol and a decrease in GABA levels. The decrease in GABA activity contributes to feelings of anxiety and stress because GABA's normal calming effect on the nervous system is reduced. This occurs alongside an increase in stress hormones like cortisol, creating an imbalance that can lead to heightened stress and anxiety.

The impact of self-leadership extends beyond individual performance. Companies with leaders who demonstrate strong self-leadership tend to have more engaged employees, lower turnover rates, higher job satisfaction, more self-efficacy, and better team and overall performance.[26] This is the true power of self-leadership—the ability to create positive change that extends far beyond yourself, one neuron at a time.

# U = UNDERSTANDING

## LEADER INTELLIGENCE

# 4

# INFERNO IN PARADISE:
# LEADERSHIP STYLES FORGED IN CRISIS

The sun had barely dipped below the horizon, painting the Acapulco sky in a breathtaking array of oranges and pinks. The rhythmic crash of waves against the shore provided a deceptively soothing backdrop to the vibrant energy pulsating through the air. It was March 2008, the peak of spring break season, and as the destination manager for student-travel provider StudentCity, I had transformed Acapulco from Mexican paradise into the ultimate party destination.

Little did I know that in a matter of hours, this paradise would become a burning hellhole, testing every ounce of my leadership abilities, and forever changing the lives of thousands.

## TRANSFORMATIONAL
## LEADERSHIP: CRAFTING THE DREAM

Years before the inferno, I had spent huge chunks of my life traveling from Boston to Acapulco, negotiating with local vendors, securing exclusive deals for everything from beach parties to MTV Spring Break concerts. I collaborated tirelessly with the tourism board, ensuring that our yearly migration of college students boosted the local economy and left a positive impact on the community.

When I first became destination manager of Acapulco in early 2002, our company sold only five hundred spring break packages to that destination. I saw the potential to reinvigorate the destination to its once former glory. To achieve this goal would take an entire transformation of the destination design, and a transformation of our organization toward a risky expansion.

I am a born extrovert with an extraordinarily high openness to new experiences, a high proactiveness toward and tolerance for risk taking, and a propensity to put myself into leadership positions. I was made comfortable with change thanks to a childhood of moving from trailer parks to Section 8 housing projects—due to the death of friends and family— and to a huge amount of childhood trauma; and I made it this far because I believe—and have been proven correct—in human power to achieve beyond their wildest imaginations, to exceed their own expectations for how well and how much they can achieve. Put all that together, *et violà*, I am a transformational leader.

As a transformational leader, I have learned that true success comes from inspiring others to see beyond the immediate and strive for something greater. Transformational leadership is a style that inspires and motivates followers to exceed their own self-interests for the good of the organization.[27] It involves creating a compelling vision, fostering a sense of purpose, and empowering individuals to reach their full potential. Transformational leadership is made up of four components:[28]

- *Idealized Influence*: Leaders act as role models, demonstrating high ethical standards and inspiring trust and respect in their followers.

I knew that to truly transform Acapulco's spring break scene, we needed to be more than just party planners. We had to be stewards of the community. I spent countless hours meeting with local vendors and tourism officials, not just to secure deals, but to understand how we could make a positive impact.

My passion for transforming Acapulco was contagious, and this was likely due to mirror neurons at work. When I'd enthusiastically share our vision or demonstrate how to close a sale, my team's mirror neurons were likely firing and adrenaline was flowing in their veins, allowing them to not just understand, but feel my excitement and determination. This neural mirroring helped spread my energy and drive throughout the organization.

- *Inspirational Motivation*: Leaders communicate a clear and inspiring vision, motivating followers to work toward a shared goal.

  I painted a vivid picture of what Acapulco could become—not just a party destination, but a place of transformation for young travelers. I created vision, mission, and value statements to make Acapulco the number one spring break destination in the company. "Imagine Acapulco as the ultimate spring break experience," I said, "where students create memories that last a lifetime and gain a deeper appreciation for Mexican culture." This was transformational leadership in action—inspiring my team with a shared vision that's bigger than any individual, empowering them to create an unforgettable experience for our student travelers, and then motivating them to work tirelessly to make that vision a reality.

By aligning our company goals with personal growth opportunities, I engaged the anterior cingulate cortex of my team members. This brain region, crucial for decision-making and emotional regulation, was likely highly active as team members saw how their personal success intertwined with our collective mission.

- *Intellectual Stimulation*: Leaders encourage creativity and critical thinking, challenging the status quo and fostering innovation.

   I challenged my team to think beyond the conventional spring break formula. We brainstormed innovative ideas, from cultural immersion trips to volunteer opportunities. My goal was to inspire others to ask the right questions and empower them to find innovative solutions. "Let's design a twenty-four-hour program that pushes the boundaries of what's possible," I'd challenge them to think critically, creatively, and strategically. My team and I meticulously designed an epic twenty-four-hour debauchery program that catered specifically to living every second to its wildest maximum.

   This type of cognitive engagement can stimulate learning processes in the brain, potentially enhancing our ability to adapt to new information and improve memory formation. While I couldn't guarantee that this challenge directly affected glutamate levels, my purpose was to stimulate cognitive processes that involve glutamate.

- *Individualized Consideration*: Leaders provide support and mentorship to each individual, recognizing their unique needs and potential.

I recognized that each team member had distinctive strengths and potential. As national sales director, I personally trained over 2,500 sales representatives, tailoring my approach to everyone's needs. Because every person is different and leads differently, we placed them with a more senior manager to equip them with the tools and knowledge to sell and manage their teams in accordance with their unique skills, motivations, experiences, and natural-born leader abilities.

When I spent time personally training employees, I was building trust and strengthening our relationships. These positive interactions likely contributed to a sense of connection and belonging within the team, systems related to the bonding hormone oxytocin. As a result, team members may have become more receptive to our shared vision and more committed to our goals. While we directly influence brain chemistry, positive social interactions can support overall well-being and team cohesion.

I consistently recognized and celebrated individual contributions within my team. When I offered specific praise, such as saying, "Your innovative ideas are making Acapulco the ultimate spring break destination," I boosted team morale and motivation, systems that are related to serotonin. This approach encouraged my team members to feel valued and appreciated, driving them to continue pushing boundaries and exceeding expectations. The sense of significance from such recognition acted as a powerful motivator in our workplace.

My goal was to create—and I succeeded in creating—a positive, supportive work environment that brought out the best in my team members. This approach not only drove sales but also fostered a passionate and committed team. We had grown from hosting a few hundred students to over five thousand each week for five consecutive weeks. Acapulco had become synonymous with spring break, a rite of passage for college students seeking sun, fun, and adventure.

## TRANSACTIONAL LEADERSHIP: COORDINATING THE RESPONSE

As a transformational leader, I had always thrived on inspiring others and building deep, meaningful connections with my team. As it turns out, my overexuberance for life doesn't resonate with everyone. Some employees distanced themselves from my enthusiastic, mission-driven style. They weren't interested in forging emotional bonds or putting in extra hours for the greater cause. Nope, all they wanted was to come in, do their nine-to-five job, and go home. No more, no less.

WTF? Didn't everyone want to be part of something bigger? To the higher-up executives I turned for advice. "Why don't these folks buy in to what we are trying to build? They don't care," I said to Maurizio, the owner.

Maurizio replied, "Yes, they do care. And, they have lives outside of the office that don't allow for overtime. Maybe they are just introverted or have a lot going on with family and don't have the emotional space to build new personal relationships. In any case, we need them to do what work they can. Plus, they are high-quality contributors, so don't knock them just because they do not want to be your friend. You are their boss, and your job is to get them to do their job."

Huh? I get it now. We pay them to do a thing, and they do that thing. We need all kinds of employees and relationships to achieve our goals. I quickly understood that employees who viewed work relationships as purely transactional were still crucial to our operation. I needed to find a way to lead them effectively, even if they didn't respond to my transformational approach.

That is when I explored the concept of transactional leadership. This style was all about clear expectations, defined roles, and rewards for performance. It was a straightforward exchange: I pay you for the work you do, and you get rewarded for meeting or exceeding targets. No emotional investment required. Transactional leadership is a style that focuses on the exchange between leaders and followers, wherein leaders set clear goals, provide rewards for performance, and monitor progress.[29] There are four potential elements:

- *Contingent Reward*: Leaders provide rewards in exchange for meeting specific goals or performance standards.

  Clear goals and expectations engage the prefrontal cortex, the brain's center for planning and goal-directed behavior. Employees became more focused and strategic in their approach to work. The nucleus accumbens, part of the brain's reward circuit, lights up when expectations are met and rewards received. This created a positive feedback loop, encouraging continued high performance.

By creating a clear cause-effect relationship between performance and rewards, I was tapping into the brain's motivation and rewards system. Our reward system, which involves various neurotransmitters including dopamine, endorphins, serotonin, GABA, and glutamate (the brain's primary excitatory neurotransmitter) plays a crucial role in learning and motivation. While we can't directly control or measure neurotransmitter activity in everyday workplace situations, research suggests that clear, attainable goals and consistent rewards can enhance employee engagement and performance by reinforcing desired behaviors.

Bonuses were offered: "If you meet your monthly quota of fifty bookings, you'll receive a 5 percent bonus."

- *Management By Exception (Active):* Leaders actively monitor for deviations from standards and take corrective action when necessary.

  I also had to be mindful of the potential increase in amygdala activity. The stress of meeting performance targets could trigger the brain's fear center, which shuts down productivity. To mitigate this, I proactively tracked progress toward goals, gave feedback to improve performance, and encouraged corrections on the spot. I would say things to address issues before they became significant problems: "John, I've noticed your conversion rate has dropped by 10 percent this week."

- *Management By Exception (Passive):* Leaders intervene only when problems become serious.

  When something was going horribly wrong, I stepped in to model the behaviors that I wanted employees to mirror.

- *Laissez-Faire:* Leaders avoid decision-making and responsibility (Bass and Avolio 1994).[30] (This was never in my repertoire, but I guarantee if you think about all the bosses you had in your life, you can identify a boss who was lazy and apathetic.)

## THE BALANCING ACT: MBA AND MAYHEM

As the spring break season kicked into high gear, I found myself in an impossible situation. Six months into my MBA program at Suffolk University in Boston, I was juggling the demands of academia with the intense responsibilities of managing the largest spring break program in our company's history.

Every Sunday night, I boarded a plane to Acapulco, my carry-on stuffed with textbooks and case studies. For five days, I immersed myself in the controlled chaos of spring break management, overseeing a staff and ensuring the safety and enjoyment of thousands of students. Friday nights I would catch a red eye back to Boston, arriving just in time for Saturday morning classes. Before I left Acapulco to attend classes in Boston, I set clear expectations for my team, ensuring that they could operate effectively during my absences. Meanwhile, I negotiated with my professors, explaining my unique situation and demonstrating my commitment to academic excellence despite the challenging circumstances. Only determination and copious amounts of tequila fueled my life in those days.

During one jaunt back to Boston, a most horrifying emergency flared up just after my flight departed Mexican airspace. At 3 a.m., the Playa Suites hotel, then home to two thousand drunk and passed out students, was set on fire.

One student traveler, stripping themselves of their night-club clothes, dowsed them with alcohol, set their attire on fire, and threw a tank-top-turned-blazing-ball down the laundry chute. Smoke billowed through corridors as flames licked up the sides of the building, casting a brilliant orange glow across the dark night sky. Moments later, one half of the building was an inferno.

Imagine scenes from the Twin Towers of the World Trade Center during the 9/11 attacks on America, but instead of being in New York City, it was in Acapulco, Mexico, on the beach at 3 a.m. That's how horrific this situation was.

Thousands of young guests, many still groggy from partying their faces off earlier that evening, stumbled from their rooms in confusion and terror; some half- and some full-naked, clutching clothes to cover themselves, others empty-handed in their rush to escape. Smoke filled the air, stinging eyes and throats, robbing them of oxygen with each breath. Panic spread like wildfire through the crowds as the reality of the situation set in. The hallways of Playa Suites erupted into chaos. Screaming in panic, coughing and crying people ran in every direction trying to identify an emergency exit through black clouds and flashing red lights that indicated a stairwell. In the stairwells, a sea of bodies pushed and shoved, driven by primal fear. Some tripped and fell, only to be helped up by strangers united in their desperation to survive. Amid the terror, acts of bravery emerged. Hotel staff and guests alike helped those struggling to evacuate, offering shoulders to lean on or carrying those unable to walk.

Outside, the scene was no less frantic. Guests spilled onto the beach, many collapsed on the sand, gulping in the fresh air. Others stood transfixed, watching in horror as flames engulfed their temporary home. The heat was intense, even from a distance. Windows shattered from the thermal stress, sending glass raining down on the evacuees below. Frantic phone calls were made to loved ones; voices choked with emotion.

## YOUR BRAIN'S NEUROLOGICAL RESPONSE TO CRISIS

During acute crises such as the Playa Suites fire and the COVID-19 pandemic, the human brain undergoes dramatic transformation, creating neurological and physiological changes and neurotransmitter release that demand a unique form of leadership. When, for example, your brain believes you are in existential threat, the brain's alarm systems ignite, with the hypothalamic-pituitary-adrenal axis triggering a biochemical cascade that floods the body with stress hormones. The amygdala, our primordial fear center, surges into overdrive, hijacking rational thought processes and potentially pushing individuals into a state of panic or paralysis.

Concurrently, the prefrontal cortex—our brain's CEO responsible for complex decision-making and impulse control—experiences a decrease in activity. This neurological shift can reduce your capacity for nuanced thinking by up to 80 percent, as measured in some stress studies.[31] Your body responds with heart rates that potentially double from their resting state, blood pressure spikes by 30 percent to 40 percent, and respiratory rates increase up to fourfold.[32] This physiological storm prepares the body for immediate action but can also impair fine motor skills and cognitive flexibility.

In this altered state of consciousness and physiology, traditional leadership approaches fail. The crisis context calls for leaders who can navigate this neurobiological tempest, cutting through fear and cognitive impairment to provide clear, actionable direction. Leaders must be adept at modulating the group's stress response, attempting to reduce cortisol levels by up to 25 percent through effective communication and decisive action.[33] They must also be able to leverage the heightened emotional state to stimulate rapid, coordinated action, turning the potential for panic into purposeful response. Leaders must provide clear, straightforward directions as followers may struggle with processing complex information, because cognitive flexibility is diminished, making it harder for individuals to switch among tasks, consider alternative solutions, or adapt to rapidly changing situations.

Leading during crisis is an exercise in real-time neurological and physiological management, where the stakes are nothing less than survival and long-term psychological well-being. Leaders often fail during crises because they do not adapt their leadership style to the neurological and physiological changes occurring in their followers' brains. Effective crisis leadership requires an understanding of these neurobiological processes, enabling leaders to modulate group stress responses and provide the type of decisive, action-oriented guidance that resonates with crisis-altered cognition.

Charismatic leadership is the most effective form of leadership during crisis. When crisis is overcome, leaders should shift into an alternative style of leadership that meets the demands of the new context and circumstances. This means, leaders must be able to change their leadership style to meet the demands of the moment, situational needs, contextual constraints, and dynamic evolving targets.[34]

## CHARISMATIC LEADERSHIP IN CRISIS

As the gravity of the situation hit me, I felt a surge of adrenaline course through my veins. This was the moment where charismatic leadership was crucial. Despite being thousands of miles away, I needed to rally my team and inspire confidence in our ability to handle this crisis.

I immediately got on a conference call with my on-site staff. I said, my voice steady and resolute, "This is what we have trained for. We have protocols in place, and I know each one of you has the skills and courage to see this through. Remember, every student in that building is counting on us. We will not let them down."

I could hear the fear in their voices turn to determination as I spoke. Charismatic leadership involves articulating an appealing vision, communicating high performance expectations, and expressing confidence in followers' abilities.[35] In this moment of crisis, these elements were crucial in motivating my team to act swiftly and decisively. Charismatic leaders are:

- *Visionary*: Charismatic leaders articulate a compelling vision for the future that inspires and motivates others.

  I jumped on that conference call like my life depended on it—because lives did depend on it. I painted a vivid picture of not just survival, but triumph. I wasn't just giving orders; I was showing them a future worth fighting for. "Listen up," I said, "When the sun rises and the smoke is clear, every student traveler will be saved. We'll send them home to be surrounded by relieved loved ones. We're standing together, exhausted, but we got this. Those students will become tomorrow's leaders, carrying this story of courage with them."

- *Passionate*: Leaders communicate their vision with enthusiasm and conviction, inspiring others to share their passion.[36]

    My energy was contagious from thousands of miles away, through a cell phone. "Everything we've worked for, every drill, every protocol—it all leads to this. By God, we will not fail!"

- *Empathetic*: Charismatic leaders understand and connect with their followers on a personal level, building trust and rapport.

    I took a breath, took my voice down a few decibels. "I know you're scared. I'm scared, too. But that fear? It's proof of how much you care, of how human you are." I connected with each of them, acknowledging their fears, their doubts. My goal was to build their trust in me, trust that we could survive and help others survive, by showing empathy toward my team. In that moment, we were a family.

- *Confident*: Charismatic leaders exude self-confidence and optimism, inspiring others to believe in themselves and their abilities.[37]

    I reflected to them a strength they might not have recognized in themselves. "You are capable of getting through this. This situation sucks and it is going to be a long night. That said, you are ready, totally prepared for emergencies. Just do what we practiced, and we will save lives. Trust your training, trust each other, and let's get this done. You've got the skills. Now use them."

During a crisis like the Playa Suites fire, understanding the neurological and physiological responses of individuals is crucial for effective leadership. The brain's immediate reaction to danger triggers a flood of stress hormones, primarily adrenaline and norepinephrine, initiating the fight-or-flight response. This surge heightens awareness but can also lead to panic and impaired decision-making.

A leader's primary task in this scenario is to create the language, systems, and processes that generate conditions where these neurochemical responses foster more adaptive group behaviors. By projecting calm and providing clear direction, a leader can create positive conditions that may help regulate stress and arousal levels in team members. This leadership approach can potentially influence the overall physiological state of followers, including factors related to the autonomic nervous system. A calm and structured environment can help mitigate excessive stress responses in team members. This regulation is key to shifting from a state of unfocused hyperarousal to one of alert, goal-directed attention. By understanding and applying these neurological principles, leaders can significantly improve group outcomes in crisis situations. This approach transforms leadership from mere authority to a form of applied neuroscience, directly influencing the cognitive and emotional states of those being led.

As I stood there, facing the crisis head-on, the team needed to know that I cared, and so I attempted to activate team members' anterior insular cortex by showing empathy and compassion, both given and received. I knew I had to kick their systems into high gear with an adrenaline (epinephrine) surge without sending them spiraling into panic. This hormone, released by the adrenal glands, prepares the body for action by increasing heart rate, elevating blood pressure, and enhancing alertness. At the same time, I didn't want to freak them out in an already bad situation. I wanted to stimulate the release of GABA, the inhibitory neurotrans-mitter that reduces neuronal excitability; serotonin to pro-mote self-control; and oxytocin, which promotes trust and cooperation. In that situation, my goal was to create condi-tions that fostered a positive neurochemical state where my team was alert and energized (thanks to controlled levels of adrenaline and norepinephrine) but not overwhelmed (due to the calming effects of GABA, serotonin, and oxytocin). This balanced state created optimal performance under pres-sure—team members were focused, quick to respond, yet able to think clearly and work cooperatively.

## SERVANT LEADERSHIP: EMPOWERING THE GROUND TEAM

As I coordinated efforts from afar, I realized that true lead-ership in this situation required trusting and empowering those on the ground. This is where servant leadership came into play, a style that focuses on the growth and well-being of people and the communities to which they belong.[38] Servant leaders do the following:

- *Listening*: Servant leaders actively listen to their follow-ers, seeking to understand their needs and concerns.

- *Empathy*: They show genuine care and concern for their followers, understanding their perspectives and feelings.

- *Healing*: They help followers to heal from past hurts and traumas, creating a safe and supportive environment.

- *Awareness*: They are self-aware and mindful of their own strengths and weaknesses.

- *Persuasion*: They use persuasion rather than coercion to influence others, building consensus and buy-in.

- *Conceptualization*: They think beyond day-to-day realities, envisioning a better future for their organization.

- *Foresight*: They anticipate future challenges and opportunities, making informed decisions based on their understanding of the past and present.

- *Stewardship*: They see themselves as stewards of their organization, responsible for its long-term health and well-being.

- *Commitment To The Growth Of People*: They invest in the development of their followers, helping them to grow both personally and professionally.

- *Building Community*: They foster a sense of community and belonging among their followers, creating a supportive and collaborative environment.

Kristen, who was working staff on site in Acapulco, took charge of the emergency procedures for the next twenty-four hours while I, stuck in the Houston airport, could not, through influence or threat, find an airplane seat back to Acapulco. Several thousand student travelers would be saved while the fire ravaged the building. While I was stuck in transit, she took charge of the emergency procedures. I made it clear to the team that Kristen had my full support and authority to make decisions on the ground.

"Kristen, I trust you completely. You know the situation better than anyone right now. Make the calls you need to make. The team is yours to lead."

This act of empowerment, a key tenet of servant leadership, allowed Kristen to respond to the rapidly evolving situation without hesitation. She discarded the safety manual I had written, recognizing that it was inadequate for the unprecedented nature of this crisis. Instead, she relied on her intuition and the relationships we had built with local authorities to coordinate a massive evacuation effort.

As a servant leader, Kristen created a caring and supportive environment that sought to trigger a surge of oxytocin, binding her and the team together in mutual confidence and loyalty. The anterior insular cortex lit up in each team member's brain as empathy and compassion flowed freely between leader and follower, a two-way street of understanding and support.

Her approach seemed to activate their vagus nerves, soothing frayed nerves and cultivating a sense of safety amid the chaos. This neurological calm allowed their prefrontal cortices to engage fully in creative problem-solving and decisive action as they embraced their newfound autonomy. All the while, GABA, nature's own tranquilizer, surged through their systems, dampening anxiety and fostering a collective sense of calm determination.

## THE UNIVERSAL LEADERSHIP PRINCIPLE:
## COORDINATE AND COLLABORATE

As the crisis unfolded, the universal leadership principle of "coordinate and collaborate" became our mantra. This principle, which emphasizes the importance of working effectively with diverse stakeholders, was critical in managing the complex web of interactions necessary to resolve the crisis. Our team coordinated with a dizzying array of entities:

- local fire departments and emergency services
- hospitals and medical staff
- police for crowd control and investigation
- hotel management for evacuation and damage assessment
- other local hotels for emergency accommodations
- airlines for potential emergency flights
- US embassy for support and communication with families
- local government officials for resources and permissions
- media outlets for accurate reporting and updates

Each of these relationships required a different approach, showcasing the need for versatility in leadership styles. With emergency services, we needed to be clear and directive. With government officials, diplomatic and persuasive. With the media, transparent yet controlled.

When I finally managed to return to Acapulco, the scene that greeted me was surreal. The once-vibrant Playa Suites stood as a charred reminder of how quickly paradise can turn to hell. Upon my return, Kristen, exhausted, with black soot still covering her rosy, red cheeks, humbly handed me the bullhorn to continue on in the effort she had deftly handled.

Over the next ninety-six hours, every emergency response unit in Acapulco would eventually participate in the fire repression and student relocation effort. American news channels (e.g., CNN) covered the story, weaving in videos taken from cell phones. A calamity of monumental proportion, caused by a single act by a single person, had been averted through heroic acts too many to count.

We worked tirelessly to relocate students, coordinate with parents, manage media inquiries, and begin the long process of understanding what had happened and how to prevent it in the future.

This phase called for a return to transformational leadership. We needed to inspire hope, chart a path forward, and help our team and the students process the trauma they had experienced.

I organized daily briefings, not just to share information, but to acknowledge the emotional toll of the event. "What you've all been through is extraordinary," I told the assembled staff and students. "It's okay to feel shaken, angry, or scared. We're here for each other, and together, we'll get through this."

We set up counseling services, organized group activities to help process the event, and worked closely with local authorities to ensure everyone felt safe and supported.

## LEADERSHIP FAILURES IN THE FACE OF A GLOBAL CRISIS: A SCATHING ANALYSIS OF THE COVID-19 RESPONSE

The COVID-19 pandemic exposed a catastrophic failure of leadership across governments, organizations, communities, and every other plane of human existence. It was obvious that leaders were so under skilled and unprepared, that the unknown unknown brought to the surface their devastating lack of adaptability, foresight, and basic competence.

While the Acapulco fire was an extreme example, it high-lighted how different leadership styles are necessary in various situations, in everyday life and during crisis. Effective crisis leadership isn't just about managing external challenges, but also about leading oneself. The ability to remain calm under pressure, make decisions with incomplete information, and inspire confidence in others are all crucial skills that are put to the test in crisis situations. The key is recognizing which style is needed in a given situation and having the flexibility to adapt accordingly.

## TRANSFORMATIONAL LEADERSHIP: A VOID WHERE VISION SHOULD HAVE BEEN

Instead of inspiring hope and articulating a compelling future, many leaders wallowed in denial and misinformation. They failed to grasp the magnitude of the crisis, leaving their followers directionless and scared. Effective transformational leaders should have painted a clear picture of a postpandemic world, outlining steps to get there while acknowledging the challenges ahead.

Transformational leadership is crucial when setting long-term goals and inspiring teams to achieve more than they thought possible. In a corporate setting, this might involve articulating a bold new vision for the company or encouraging employees to think innovatively about long-standing problems.

## TRANSACTIONAL LEADERSHIP:
## INCONSISTENCY AND CHAOS REIGNED SUPREME

The implementation of safety protocols was a jumbled mess of conflicting information and half measures. Leaders failed to set clear expectations or consequences, resulting in confusion and noncompliance.

A proper transactional approach would have involved crystal clear communication, consistent enforcement, and appropriate incentives for adherence to new protocols. Transactional leadership comes into play in day-to-day operations, where clear goals, rewards, and consequences help maintain order and efficiency. This could be as simple as setting clear performance metrics for a sales team or establishing deadlines for project milestones.

## CHARISMATIC LEADERSHIP:
## EMPTY WORDS AND ABSENT EMPATHY

Many leaders hid behind press releases or sporadic, tone-deaf appearances. They failed to connect emotionally with their constituents, offering platitudes instead of genuine empathy. True charismatic leadership would have involved regular, authentic communication that acknowledged fears while instilling confidence.

## SERVANT LEADERSHIP:
## SELF-INTEREST TRUMPED PUBLIC WELFARE

Instead of prioritizing public health and employee well-being, many leaders focused on short-term economic interests or political gain. They abandoned their duty to serve, leaving vulnerable populations exposed. Genuine servant leaders would have put people first, making tough decisions to protect public health even at the cost of temporary economic pain.

Servant leadership is particularly effective in fostering a positive organizational culture and developing future leaders. This might involve mentoring programs, prioritizing employee well-being, or creating opportunities for team members to grow and take on new responsibilities.

## WHY YOU SHOULD CARE
## ABOUT LEADERSHIP STYLES

The Acapulco fire was a crucible that forged my understanding of leadership in ways that no textbook or case study ever could. It taught me that true leadership is not about adhering to a single style or approach, but about having the wisdom to know which style is needed in a given moment and the flexibility to adapt quickly.

In the years since that harrowing night, I've carried these lessons with me in every leadership role I've undertaken. Whether I'm leading a team through a high-stakes business negotiation or helping a nonprofit navigate a funding crisis, I draw upon the full spectrum of leadership styles I honed in the face of that inferno.

The fire also taught me the immense responsibility that

comes with leadership. Every decision, every word, can have profound impacts on the lives of others. This realization has instilled in me a deep sense of humility and a commitment to continuous learning and self-improvement.

As we navigate an increasingly complex and unpredictable world, the ability to lead effectively through crises—whether they be literal fires or metaphorical ones—will only become more crucial. The leaders who will thrive are those who can blend different leadership styles seamlessly, who can inspire and direct, empower and decide, all while maintaining their own emotional equilibrium.

The Acapulco fire was not just a test of my leadership skills; it was a forge that shaped my very understanding of what leadership means. In the dance of flames and the chorus of sirens, in the faces of terrified students and determined staff, I learned lessons that no classroom could ever teach. And for that, despite the terror and trauma of those days, I am profoundly grateful.

In the postmortem of that event, I began to look deeper into myself, self-diagnosing my psychological and emotional states before and after the event, and how well or poorly I performed during the most important ninety-six hours of leadership in my life. There was a sense that my brain was rewired, and it was obvious that so too had the brains of my staff been rewired. This was the beginnings of my search into the neurological effects of leadership, and into the discovery of whether a leader could influence the combination of information, behaviors, emotions, and neurotransmitters of followers in real time, to influence the behaviors necessary to get work done with and through people.

Because leaders who nimbly shift among multiple leadership styles are able to create more holistic brain engagement and to foster creativity, emotional connection, and intrinsic motivation, they potentially indirectly affect neurological responses. Understanding these neurological responses allows us to see leadership not just as a set of behaviors, but as a powerful tool for creating optimal brain states in our teams. By fostering trust, significance, empathy, purposeful decision-making, and stress reduction, we create an environment where people naturally perform at their best.

Leaders who understand these neurological principles can intentionally shape followers' actions to trigger positive brain states. It is not about manipulation, but about creating the conditions where people's brains are primed for growth, creativity, and exceptional performance. This is the true power of leadership—aligning our actions with the natural workings of the human brain to unlock the full potential of our teams.

The pandemic revealed a stunning lack of leader abilities and horrific global coordination and collaboration. Leaders retreated into nationalism and finger-pointing instead of collaborative problem-solving. Effective crisis management required seamless cooperation across borders, sharing of resources and information, and a united front against a common enemy.

The pandemic exposed the dire consequences of inadequate leadership. As we move forward, we must demand and develop leaders who can navigate complexity, inspire trust, and prioritize collective well-being over narrow interests. The next crisis is not a matter of if, but when. We cannot afford another leadership failure of this magnitude.

All these challenges lead me to call for radical reform in postpandemic leadership. In the wake of these grotesque and epic failures, effective leadership today must embrace multiple styles and approaches that meet the demands of the context and followers' needs for supportive leadership:

- *Empathetic Action*: Understanding the human impact of decisions is crucial. Leaders must balance data-driven decisions with compassion.

- *Adaptive Expertise*: Leaders must be able to pivot quickly, learning and applying new information in real time.

- *Global Mindset*: Isolationism is a death sentence in a connected world. Leaders must think and act globally, even in local contexts.

- *Scientific Literacy*: Leaders must understand and respect scientific consensus, integrating expert knowledge into decision-making.

- *Resilience Planning*: Instead of reactive crisis management, leaders must proactively build resilient systems capable of withstanding future shocks.

- *Ethical Backbone*: Leaders must have the courage to make unpopular decisions when public welfare is at stake. The ability to do and say the right thing, especially when popular trends violate your moral compass, is the core of being an authentic leader.

- *Transparent Communication*: No more sugarcoating or obfuscation. Leaders must provide clear, consistent, and honest information.

Leaders today must recognize the urgent need to develop crucial skills that have been exposed as weak in the postpandemic landscape. These essential leadership muscles—encompassing empathetic action, adaptive expertise, global mindset, scientific literacy, resilience planning, ethical decision-making, and transparent communication—require deliberate strengthening and consistent exercise.

By developing these leadership muscles, we can create workplace conditions that positively influence motivation to perform. Motivation to perform refers to the internal and external forces that drive individuals to achieve high levels of performance in their work. In the postpandemic context, motivation to perform has all but evaporated as organizations struggle to manage new ways of working, increased uncertainty, and evolving employee expectations.

Strong leader muscles enable us to provide the autonomy, purpose, well-being support, recognition, and sense of belonging that drive employee engagement and high performance. As we strengthen these capabilities, we become better equipped to navigate complexity, inspire trust, and prioritize collective well-being. This multifaceted approach to leadership development is not optional but imperative in our volatile world. Only by consciously building these leader muscles can we create the resilient, motivated, and high-performing teams necessary to tackle future challenges and drive organizational success.

# 5

# LEADER INTELLIGENCE: REAL AND ARTIFICIAL

As a leadership expert and consultant, I found myself at a real and AI crossroads. My clients were increasingly asking about AI and its implications for leadership. I realized that to continue being an effective guide for leaders, I needed to develop expertise about AI-enhanced leadership. This journey led me to explore key areas where AI can revolutionize leadership while maintaining the essential human relational and decision-making elements. This chapter is dedicated to sharing how I learned to leverage AI to equip my clients with cutting-edge technology while emphasizing the irreplaceable human elements of leadership.

My journey began with a simple question: How can AI technology improve the quality of our life and leadership by amplifying our uniquely human qualities rather than attempting to replace them?

## AI-ENHANCED LEADERSHIP COMMUNICATION

Effective communication is a crucial leadership skill, and AI can help leaders communicate more effectively with their teams.

**Implementation**

Implement AI-powered communication analysis tools like Quantified Communications or Receptiviti. These tools can analyze written and verbal communications for clarity, tone, and potential impact. Use these tools to analyze leaders' emails, presentations, and even real-time speech during meetings. AI can provide feedback on factors like use of inclusive language, clarity of message, and emotional tone.

Implement an AI writing assistant like Grammarly Business for leaders to use when crafting important communications. This can help improve clarity and catch potential issues before messages are sent.

Use AI-powered sentiment analysis to gauge how team members are responding to leadership communications. This can help identify any disconnects between intended and received messages. Implement AI-powered translation tools for global teams. These can help ensure that leadership messages are accurately conveyed across language barriers.

Use AI to analyze the effectiveness of different communication strategies over time. It can identify which approaches resonate best with different team members or in different situations.

**Expected Outcome**

You will see improved clarity and effectiveness of leadership communications, better alignment between leader intent and team understanding, and more engaged employees. AI provides objective analysis and suggestions for improvement, while your human touch ensures that communications remain authentic and aligned with leadership style and organizational culture.

## PERSONALIZED LEADERSHIP DEVELOPMENT:
## THE AI MENTOR

Effective leadership development must be tailored to the individual, but doing this at scale seemed impossible—until I discovered AI-powered learning platforms.

**Implementation**

I experimented with several platforms before settling on Docebo's AI-powered learning suite. I input my own leadership journey—my strengths, weaknesses, learning style, and career aspirations. AI crafted a personalized development plan that was impressively accurate, suggesting resources and experiences that resonated deeply with me.

But it wasn't perfect. AI couldn't account for the emotional intelligence and soft skills that are crucial for leadership. So, I developed a hybrid approach. I now use AI to create a foundational development plan for my clients, which we then refine together, incorporating the human elements that AI can't capture.

This approach has been a game changer. My clients appreciate the data-driven foundation of their development plans, but they value even more the personal touch that comes from our one-on-one discussions about their unique challenges and aspirations.

Here are a few steps to implement AI for leader development: Start by selecting an AI-powered learning platform like Docebo or EdCast. Input comprehensive data about each leader, including their performance metrics, psychometric assessments, 360-degree feedback, and career aspirations.

AI will analyze this data to create a tailored development plan for each leader. But here's where your human touch comes in: Review each plan personally. Look for areas where the AI might have missed nuances about the individual's strengths or the organization's unique culture.

Next, set up regular check-ins with each leader. Use these sessions to discuss the AI-generated insights, but also to uncover any challenges or aspirations that the data might not capture.

Encourage leaders to log their progress and reflections in the AI system. This continuous feed of data will allow AI to adjust and refine the development plan over time.

Finally, create a mentorship program that complements the AI-driven plan. Use the AI's insights to match mentors and mentees based on complementary skills and experiences.

**Expected Outcome**

You will see more engaged leaders, faster skill development, and better alignment between individual growth and organizational needs. The combination of AI-driven insights and your human guidance will create a powerful, personalized leadership development program.

## STRATEGIC PLANNING WITH AI

Strategic planning is crucial for organizational success, and AI can enhance this process significantly. IBM's Watson decision platform is a useful tool for exploring AI-powered decision support systems to analyze complex datasets about market trends.

I input the data along with my research questions. Within minutes, Watson presented me with three potential market strategies, each with probability scores and potential pitfalls. But here's the crucial part—I didn't blindly accept Watson's top-ranked option.

Instead, I reflected on my years of experience, the nuanced understanding of market dynamics that only comes from being in the trenches. I chose the second-ranked option because I knew it aligned better with the human elements of business—consumer psychology and brand loyalty.

This experience taught me a valuable lesson: AI can crunch numbers faster than any human, but it can't replace the wisdom that comes from years of hands-on experience. I now teach my clients to use AI as a powerful input to their decision-making process, not as the decision-maker itself.

**Implementation**
Start by implementing an AI-powered strategic foresight platform like Shaping Tomorrow or Quid. Input data about your organization's current state, market conditions, and industry trends.

AI will analyze this data along with vast amounts of external information to identify emerging trends, potential disruptors, and strategic opportunities. It might generate multiple future scenarios based on different variables.

Organize a strategic planning workshop with your leadership team. Present the AI's analysis and scenarios as a starting point for discussion. Encourage leaders to question the AI's assumptions and add their own insights based on their industry experience.

Use AI-powered collaboration tools during the workshop to capture ideas and analyze their potential impact in real time. This could help prioritize initiatives and allocate resources more effectively. After the workshop, use AI to stress test the chosen strategy. It can simulate various market conditions and organizational changes to identify potential risks and opportunities. Put in place a system for regularly feeding new data into the AI platform. This will allow for continuous refinement of the strategy based on changing conditions.

*It is essential for human beings to sharpen and improve their critical, creative, and strategic thinking.*

These interconnected thinking modes are essential for effective leadership and cannot be replaced by AI. Critical thinking is the objective analysis and evaluation of information to form a judgment. Creative thinking is the ability to generate new ideas, approaches, or solutions. Strategic thinking is the ability to think long-term and develop a vision for the future. These three thinking modes are not mutually exclusive; rather, they are interconnected and complementary. Critical thinking helps leaders evaluate ideas and strategies, creative thinking generates new possibilities, and strategic thinking aligns these ideas with long-term goals. By cultivating all three modes of thinking, leaders can navigate complexity, solve problems, and drive innovation in an ever-changing world.

**Expected Outcome**
You will develop more robust, forward-looking strategies that balance data-driven insights with human vision and judgment. AI helps identify blind spots and opportunities that might be missed through traditional planning processes, while your leadership team's experience and intuition ensure the strategy is practical and aligned with organizational values.

## AI-ENHANCED PERFORMANCE REVIEWS:
## THE UNBIASED OBSERVER

Performance reviews have always been a pain point for many of my clients. Subjectivity and bias often creep in, leading to unfair evaluations. Traditional annual reviews are often subjective and do not provide actionable insights. To address this, AI can help create a more continuous, data-driven performance management process.

I experimented with 15Five's AI-enhanced performance management system. AI could quantify performance, but it couldn't capture the nuances of teamwork, creativity, or leadership potential.

So, I developed a balanced approach. I now advise my clients to use AI-generated performance data as a starting point, but to always layer it with human insight. A great performance review isn't just about the numbers—it's about understanding the story behind those numbers and helping employees grow.

**Implementation**

Start by implementing an AI-powered performance management system like 15Five or Lattice. Customize the system to track key performance indicators relevant to your organization. Train managers and employees on how to use the system for regular check-ins and feedback. Encourage them to input qualitative data along with quantitative metrics.

AI will analyze this ongoing stream of data to provide real-time performance insights. It might identify trends in performance, flag potential issues, or highlight areas for recognition. Coach managers on how to use these AI-generated insights in their regular one-on-one meetings with team members. Remind them that the AI's analysis is a tool to enhance, not replace, their own observations and judgment. Use the AI's aggregated data to inform broader talent management decisions, like identifying high potentials or areas where additional training is needed across the organization.

### Expected Outcome

You will see more engaged employees, better alignment between individual and organizational goals, and more informed talent management decisions. The continuous nature of this AI-enhanced process allows for more timely interventions and recognition.

## AI-DRIVEN CONFLICT RESOLUTION

Conflict in the workplace is inevitable, but AI can help manage it more effectively. Later in the book we dedicate a full chapter to winning conflict.

### Implementation

Develop or acquire an AI system that can analyze conflict situations. This system should be able to process information about the nature of the conflict, the parties involved, and the context in which it occurred.

Train human resources (HR) professionals and managers on how to input conflict data into the system. This might include descriptions of the conflict, personality assessments of those involved, and relevant organizational context. AI will analyze this data and suggest potential resolution strategies based on successful outcomes in similar situations. It might recommend specific mediation techniques or communication strategies.

Here's where your expertise comes in: Review the AI's suggestions and adapt them based on your understanding of the individuals involved and the organization's culture. Use the AI's insights as a starting point for crafting a personalized conflict resolution approach. Coach managers or mediators on how to implement this approach, emphasizing the importance of emotional intelligence and active listening alongside the AI-suggested strategies. After each conflict resolution process, input the outcomes back into the AI system. This will help it learn and refine its suggestions over time.

**Expected Outcome**
You will see faster, more effective conflict resolution, leading to improved team dynamics and productivity. AI provides a structured approach, while your human touch ensures the resolution process is sensitive to the nuances of each situation.

## AI-ENHANCED EMPLOYEE ENGAGEMENT

Employee engagement refers to the emotional commitment and connection an employee has to their organization and its goals. It is characterized by the following:

- *Enthusiasm For Work*: Engaged employees are passionate about their jobs and find fulfillment in their tasks.

- *Dedication To The Organization's Mission*: They believe in and actively contribute to the company's objectives.

- *Discretionary Effort*: Engaged employees often go above and beyond their basic job requirements.

- *Positive Attitude*: They maintain an optimistic outlook and constructive approach to challenges.

- *Willingness To Collaborate*: They work well with colleagues and contribute to a positive team environment.

- *Loyalty*: Engaged employees are more likely to stay with the organization long-term.

- *Proactivity*: They take initiative in problem-solving and innovation.

- *Alignment With Company Values*: Their personal values often align with those of the organization.

- *Customer Focus*: They are committed to delivering high-quality service or products to customers.

- *Continuous Improvement*: Engaged employees seek opportunities for personal and professional growth.

High levels of employee engagement are associated with increased productivity, improved customer satisfaction, and better overall organizational performance. It is a key factor in creating a positive workplace culture and achieving business success.

**Implementation**
Begin by implementing an AI-powered employee engagement platform like Viva Glint or Qualtrics. These platforms can continuously gather and analyze employee feedback through various channels.

Set up regular pulse surveys that ask employees about their job satisfaction, work environment, and overall engagement. AI will analyze these responses in real time, identifying trends and potential issues.

Train managers to use the AI-generated insights in their team management. AI might flag teams or individuals with declining engagement scores, suggesting areas for intervention. Use the AI's natural language processing capabilities to analyze open-ended feedback and identify common themes or concerns that might not be captured in structured survey questions.

Implement an AI-powered chatbot that employees can use to voice concerns or ask questions anonymously. This can provide valuable insights into issues that employees might be hesitant to raise directly.

Regularly review the AI's aggregated insights with your leadership team. Use these to inform organization-wide initiatives to improve engagement.

### Expected Outcome

You will see improved employee engagement, faster identification and resolution of issues, and a more responsive organizational culture. AI provides continuous, data-driven insights, while your human leadership ensures that actions taken in response are empathetic and aligned with organizational values.

## AI-ENHANCED ONBOARDING

Effective onboarding is a comprehensive process designed to integrate new employees into an organization successfully. It goes beyond simple orientation and paperwork, aiming to fully immerse new hires in the company's culture, processes, and expectations. Key elements of effective onboarding include

- clear communication of job responsibilities and expectations
- an introduction to company culture, values, and mission
- provision of necessary tools and resources
- structured training programs tailored to the role
- assignment of a mentor or buddy for guidance
- regular check-ins and feedback sessions
- gradual introduction to key stakeholders and team members
- a clear outline of performance goals and metrics
- opportunities for early wins and contributions
- introduction to company policies and procedures

Effective onboarding typically extends beyond the first few days or weeks, often lasting several months to ensure full integration. It aims to reduce time to productivity, improve job satisfaction, and increase retention rates. By providing a thorough, well-planned onboarding experience, organizations can set new employees up for long-term success and engagement.

## Implementation

Implement an AI-powered onboarding platform like Enboarder or Click Boarding. These can create personalized onboarding experiences based on the new hire's role, background, and learning style.

Use AI to create a customized onboarding schedule for each new employee. This might include tailored training modules, meet-and-greet sessions with relevant team members, and gradual introduction to job responsibilities. Implement an AI chatbot that new employees can use to ask questions about company policies, procedures, or their role. This provides instant support and reduces the burden on HR and managers.

Use AI to track each new hire's progress through their onboarding journey. It can flag if someone is falling behind or struggling with certain aspects, allowing for timely intervention. Implement AI-powered gamification elements in the onboarding process. This can make the process more engaging and help reinforce key information.

Use AI to analyze feedback from new hires about their onboarding experience. This can help continuously refine and improve the process.

## Expected Outcome

You will see faster integration of new employees, improved retention rates, and higher job satisfaction among new hires. AI provides a personalized, efficient onboarding experience, while your human touch ensures that new employees feel genuinely welcomed and supported.

## AI-POWERED SKILL GAP ANALYSIS
## AND TRAINING RECOMMENDATIONS

In today's rapidly changing business environment, identifying and addressing skill gaps is crucial for organizational success. A skills gap refers to the disparity between the skills employers need and the skills their workforce actually possesses. It can occur due to technological advancements, changing market demands, or inadequate training and education systems. Skills gaps can significantly affect an organization's productivity, competitiveness, and ability to innovate.

A leadership skills gap specifically relates to the deficiency in crucial leadership competencies within an organization's management team. This can include shortcomings in areas such as strategic thinking, emotional intelligence, change management, or effective communication. Leadership skills gaps can severely hinder an organization's ability to navigate challenges, inspire teams, and drive growth in today's complex business environment.

### Implementation

Start by implementing an AI-powered skills intelligence platform like Degreed or Pluralsight Skills. These platforms can analyze your workforce's current skills and compare them to industry benchmarks and future skill requirements.

Input data about your organization's strategic goals and anticipated future projects. AI will use this information, along with analysis of industry trends, to predict future skill needs. Use AI to analyze each employee's current skill set, learning style, and career aspirations. It can then generate personalized learning recommendations to address individual skill gaps.

Implement an AI-powered learning management system

that can deliver personalized training content based on identified skill gaps. This might include a mix of online courses, microlearning modules, and recommended on-the-job experiences. Use AI to track learning progress and skill development over time. It can provide real-time updates to employees and managers and adjust learning recommendations based on progress.

Regularly review the AI's aggregated insights about organizational skill gaps with your leadership team. Use these insights to inform broader talent development strategies and potential hiring needs.

### Expected Outcome

You will see more targeted skill development, better alignment between employee skills and organizational needs, and improved readiness for future challenges. AI provides data-driven insights and personalized learning paths, while your human leadership ensures that skill development aligns with broader organizational strategy and individual career aspirations.

## THE HUMAN TOUCH IN AN AI WORLD

As I integrated these AI tools into my leadership consultancy, I had a profound realization: AI is an incredibly powerful ally, but it is not a replacement for human leadership. AI can process data at lightning speed, identify patterns, and make predictions. But it can't replace a leader's empathy, ethical judgment, or ability to inspire.

I have come to see my role as a bridge between the world of AI and the world of human leadership. I help my clients leverage AI to enhance their capabilities, while always emphasizing the irreplaceable value of human touch.

For instance, when I am coaching a CEO on strategic decision-making, we might use an AI platform to analyze market trends and competitive landscapes. But the final decision always comes down to human judgment—weighing the AI insights against the company's values, culture, and long-term vision.

When I am helping a team improve their collaboration, we might use AI to analyze their communication patterns. But the real breakthroughs come from the human-led discussions about trust, vulnerability, and shared purpose.

My journey into AI-enhanced leadership has reinforced my belief in the power of human leadership. AI makes human skills more important than ever. As AI takes over more routine tasks, uniquely human skills like emotional intelligence, creativity, and ethical reasoning become even more crucial.

That is why I always emphasize the following to my clients: Use AI to inform your decisions, but let your humanity guide them. Use AI to free up time from routine tasks, so you can focus more on connecting with your team, understanding their unique needs, and inspiring them to excel.

The future of leadership is here, and it is more human than ever. It's about using AI as a powerful tool to amplify our human capabilities, not replace them. It's about becoming better humans, not trying to compete with machines.

To all the leaders out there, I say this: Embrace AI, learn its capabilities, but never forget that your greatest strength is your humanity. The best leaders of the future will be those who can dance skillfully with AI, knowing when to lean on its insights and when to trust their human instincts. Remember that AI is a tool to augment human leadership, not replace it. The most successful implementations will be those that skillfully blend AI's analytical power with human empathy, judgment, critical thinking, creative thinking, and strategic thinking.

# S = STRATEGY

## (VISION, MISSION, VALUES, AND ABCV: ALWAYS BE CREATING VALUE)

# 6

## LIVE YOUR VISION, MISSION, AND VALUES

A rough-and-tumble Tommy Deptula caught the eye of my mom a few years before he would join the ranks of the doomed to Vietnam War. Lighting his Marlboro Reds with a red-hot stainless-steel Zippo and a coolness that emanated from his ease of manner, he'd ask Mom: "Pass me the EZ-Widers. Let's roll one up. Want me to play covers of Carlos Santana on my guitar?"

Mom and Tommy were married before he would volunteer for the Army. Like so many other things, their marriage died the moment the war became a part of their lives. Shortly thereafter, Tommy was shipped off to Vietnam, found himself in a jungle listening to the roar of warplanes overhead and artillery fire on the ground. Feeling the ground shake under his feet, soon followed a dousing of Agent Orange, soaking his uniform from head to toe. He would return home a different man, terrorized by the horrors of war, reliving vile memories of fallen friends shot or blown up just feet away from him. An evil combination stirred inside him: as the venomous psychological trauma haunted him the toxic Agent Orange began its dirty work.

Upon his return, nothing was the same in their marriage. The inevitable divorce broke them apart soon after.

The problem wasn't love. At the end of his tour, Tommy didn't know himself and my mom didn't know the battered man he became. Commitment to one another, as people, though, would never sever. They remained deeply connected.

Shortly after the divorce, Mom shared the news of her pregnancy with Tommy. By this time, Tommy had remarried and was caring for his new bride and brood. A man of great character, who lived into his values, he let his moral compass guide his every move. Knowing the complications of me not having a bio daddy on scene, Tommy did something so noble, selfless, magnanimous, and benevolent, that it changed the world in which we live today. His romance for my mother had perished, but his love of her as a person lived; and anything that came from her he loved as if it were her. "I will help you raise this baby, love him and take care of him as my own," Tommy said. Tommy's love was so grand that it radiated from inside his heart to inside Mom's belly. From the moment I was born, Tommy was the only father that I ever *really* knew.

A gentle giant, Tommy would pick me up by my tiny baby hips and thrust me high in the air. He'd lie on his back and raise his legs straight to the ceiling, hoisting me atop his feet to play airplane, a game I now play with my own children. His home was the place that smelled of kielbasa and sauer-kraut...*um-hmm...*yummy pierogis to soak up all the juices left glistening in cast-iron skillets. As I grew, so too did Tommy's family, and he welcomed his own son and daughter. Far as I knew, these people were my actual brother and sister. Moving among various caretakers was just life—nothing "modern" or new age parenting about it; and no one ever made me feel like an outsider to their bloodline.

Camping, crabbing, and fishing trips gave Tommy a plat-form to teach us kids about the three *p*'s: planning, preparation, and patience. Anyone who has ever accomplished getting a group of children—or group of people—ready and out of the house knows this is a major life achievement. Tommy knew the cadence and process of leading those who were unlikely to listen to leadership. He understood the nuances of leading a family. Getting his family to follow without incident was as simple as creating, communicating, and getting buy-in on a plan that was easy to understand and had value to each person. Effective leaders, as Tommy assuredly was, get input on vision, mission, and values, deftly garnering buy-in along the discovery process. Leaders find ways for each person to contribute value—at the level to which they were able to contribute—prepare conditions for success, and then provide support with limitless patience as each person tries their best—and fails repeatedly—and then ultimately get the job done. As a leader in my adult life, I embrace his motto: "If you fail to plan, you plan to fail." As a child I was taught the virtues of the three *p*'s to generate the highest probability for successful completion of tasks, project, and goals.

He'd start by inviting us to give input into possible family vacations: "Where do you want to go this year for spring break?" Input received and considered, kids would be gathered in the living room, trooped up, and advised of the plans.

Tommy was a great leader of his family and applied to his family the same processes of creating clear vision, mission, and value statements to give direction, purpose, and emotional connection to the organizations he led.

Vision, mission, and values are the roadmap to success as a destination. The combination of those statements gives employees clear direction as to where they are going, why they are going there, and the set of emotional and behavioral pillars with which they can create connectivity and guide behaviors.

Vision, mission, and value statements unify; they allow everyone to march in one direction and create cohesion in the work.

- *Vision* refers to the ideal outcome, what the world will look like once the organization achieves its mission.
  - Where we were going, always reminding us that the status quo needed to change: "It's been a long winter of staying inside. We need to be outdoors and break out of hibernation. I see a fun weekend ahead."

- *Mission* refers to the organization's reason for existing, its purpose for doing the specific work it does.
  - How we achieve the vision: "We're going camping, crabbing, and fishing at the beach."

- *Values* refer to the set of emotional and behavioral beliefs about how the organization and its employees ought to or should behave.[39]
  - In the words sometimes attributed to Mahatma Gandhi: "Your beliefs become your thoughts. Your thoughts become your words. Your words become your actions. Your actions become your habits. Your habits become your values. Your values become your destiny."
  - Tommy helped us understand why what we were doing was important: "Families who play together stay together."

- *ABCV—Always Be Creating Value*: "Who's coming with me? Crabs or no crabs, the best ice cream is at the beach." *Bathing suits and campfires are better than basements and kerosene heaters. I'm in.*

Tommy would start the preparation on bended knee, at our eye level, addressing each child individually. He said, "You are in charge of you. Your responsibility is to get ready and bring your sleeping bag. When you are fully clothed, teeth brushed, shoes on, meet me at the front door." Self-leadership was a constant theme reinforced with annoying frequency. Everyone committed to their part, each adding value for the good of the group. "What you do helps us all. Put your bag in the car and come back for more stuff," Tommy said.

Ready to explore the great outdoors, we'd prepare ... to buy some beers. Back in the 1980s, when the legal age to purchase alcohol were less enforced, Tommy would send my brother and I on beer runs to the local package store. The local purveyor of Beer-Wine-Spirits was a friendly chap who Tommy would call to advise that his boys were in route to pick up a dozen of his favorite beer, Black Label. Happy as clams, my brother and I marched two blocks down a bustling city street in a concrete jungle, walked up to the drive-in window, and took hold of a brown paper bag filled with cans of suds—an errand that would probably get a parent in deep trouble nowadays. Beers in hand, we'd load up the wagon and drive—destination unknown. Dad would figure out a campsite by opening a map and pointing to a spot. "That looks good. Whadda ya think, kids?" The anticipation of a good road trip excited me then, as now, with daydreams of possibilities.

Open roads open minds. Oh, what fun awaits. Exploring to be done. Who knows where we'll end up, and who cares? The journey *is* the destination.

Summer in Delaware is hot and humid. Greenhead flies—the kind that cause pain when they bite—mosquitos, and no-see-ums stick to your skin, trapped in a film of perspiration that covers every inch of your body. Standing on the docks, inches above the water, sun bouncing off the surface of the brackish bay, with wind that feels like you're standing in front of a hair dryer, we kids would crab for hours. There are two things you need to know about people from the mid-Atlantic: they love them some blue crabs, and parents get endless hours of entertainment for kids with a bonus of free crabs.

Tommy said, "Let me show you how to catch crabs, son. Take a piece of white string and loop it around a frozen neck bone of a chicken. It's slippery, so don't drop it into the water. Tie the loose end of the string to the dock, slowly lower it in the water. You'll know when the crab bites because the line will go tight. Yell 'crab on.' Pull the string a half centimeter at a time, tricking the crab into believing it isn't being moved at all. Someone will grab the net, and when the blue-gray outline of a crab body can be seen through the murky survey of water, slowly lower the net to the underside and back, snatching the crab from the water in one swooping motion." The process of pulling a crustacean from its mud bottom dwelling takes patience. By working with us as he showed us how to tie the line, he both empowered us to do it ourselves, and demonstrated patience with those who made mistakes.

I can't tell you how many crabs ate free chicken necks as a result of our dropping the bait into the water before the line was tied correctly. Tommy smiled and said, "OK, let's do it again." In allowing us to make mistakes, and then being patient as we learned the craft, Tommy showed how to lead others through teaching them skills and allowing them to learn without fearing a frustrated teacher. He'd do the same thing teaching us fishing knots. No more fun has ever been had than by kids running away from a pinching crab on a dock, evading and fighting off its captures in a duel for life.

"Crab on," I yelled, which created a frenzied panic for anyone who wanted to pull the crab out of the water.

"Grab the net. Get down close. Don't move too fast or you'll scare 'em away. They can see us on top of the water, don't ya know?"

"It's my turn," said one sibling.

"No, it's mine. Gimme the net," said the other. By the time fighting among siblings determined who would net the crab, these sly crustaceans would be long gone.

One fine crabbing day, in an especially brutal heat, saw the lot of us on the dock, shut out. The funk of raw chicken necks used for bait became putrid, filling our nose with stench. Swilling down the last of his Black Labels, looking at an empty bushel and sunburned kids who had begun to squabble out of boredom, Tommy said: "Kids, we're gonna give it one more shot." With all the frustration he could muster, he kicked his pocket transistor radio clear off the dock and into the water.

*Bam.* A line went tight. Then another, and another. From the moment that radio hit the water, crabs started jumping on bait, as if they had been shocked into eating. Two hours later we had caught over three dozen crabs, a kingly feast.

Before leaving the dock, but after we had been encouraged to "clean up what you mess up," Tommy casually conveyed a life lesson that my own children often hear when we go crabbing. He said, "What happened here is proof that you should never give up; no matter how frustrated you are. Those crabs were there, but we couldn't see them, and they didn't want to show themselves. Some of the greatest opportunities are like those crabs: just under the surface, but not ready to show themselves.

Keep pushing, try everything, even when you have nothing else to do, kick a radio. Now that radio cost me five dollars, but we caught two hundred dollar's worth of crabs. If I had to do it all over again, I would have kicked that radio into the water four hours earlier. You boys were working all day. We believed we were going home empty handed, but now our bushel is filled with abundance. Don't give up. Have patience. Make the effort. Opportunity is there, you just might not see it at first."

*Ouch. That crab claw just sliced my fingers open.* "You'll be fine. Let me show you how to crack the claws without bleeding all over the place," Tommy said.

"MommaCis cleans the crabs for me. Can you do it, please?"

Tommy said, "Oh, she does? I'm gonna talk to her about that. You gotta start learning now. Take this hammer. Give it a good whack. Watch out though, you'll get yellow mustard from the crab's guts all over your face if you do it too hard." Tommy and MommaCis were in cahoots in their efforts to raise me. They talked parenting strategy all the time; Tommy teaching recreation and leisurely pursuits while MommaCis dished out manners in pints and quarts.

MommaCis claimed her name as byproduct of being in the room for my first breath. While my biological mother provided a home and shelter, MommaCis gave me love, security, and bonding. As an infant, I spent so much time with Charlotte Lillian Murphy, that I called her Momma; later adding on her nickname Cis. The name stuck to her as much as I did, and rarely was there a time when I was not with her. MommaCis had no biological children of her own. She had chosen me to be her child, and God granted us both to one another. She said: "You are not of my blood, but of my heart, my choosing. You are my son."

"Go to the store and get me a pack of Menthol 100s. Here's a twenty-dollar bill," MommaCis said.

"I don't need a twenty. Cigarettes only cost three dollars," a fact I knew from having purchased her many packs of cigarettes.

She said, "Better to have too much than not enough. Always be prepared to have more than you think you'll need."

"But you always give me more than I need."

"Yes, and I always will. What happens if one day you see a deck of baseball cards with your favorite player? The value of that card alone is worth more than the cost of the pack. You'll want to buy that, won't you? Because then, you've made money by spending money," she said.

"Okay! I see your point."

MommaCis said, "Plus, you might be thirsty from your walk and want to buy a drink. What then if you have no money?"

"Alright already. Jeez. I hear ya."

The counter clerk looked at my ragged clothes and parched lips.

"Pack of Menthol 100s please."

"Sure, kid," said the clerk. He chucked the cigarettes across the counter. I don't know how, but in the 1980s' an eight-year-old kid could buy beer and cigarettes. "Looks like you could stand to wet your whistle." Both MommaCis and the clerk were right.

"I'll take a Gatorade." Next to the fridge sat a pack of baseball cards, Mike Schmidt, the Philadelphia Phillies Hall of Fame third baseman, was the first card showing through plastic wrapping—easily worth fifty times the cost of that pack. All three items made their way into a bag that the clerk handed to me with ten dollars change. Between chugs of red sugar water, I told MommaCis about the value of this baseball card. She listened with a knowing smile. Without having to lecture, MommaCis and Tommy taught me lessons that made life a lot easier and my leadership more effective:

- *Vision*: Seeing mentally where we are going gives you the ability to see what might happen in the future. You can plan and prepare around what you anticipate.

- *Mission*: To achieve what you are trying to achieve, plan and prepare for the highly probable; you must have at the ready more resources than you think are necessary.

- *Values*:
  - Teach people life and leadership lessons that help them understand how to be successful in life.
  - Train them on the specific tasks and functions, give them the information they need, and explain your expectations about how they will achieve their mission.
  - Give people the resources they need to complete the mission.

## WHY YOU SHOULD CARE ABOUT VISION, MISSION, VALUES

Tommy and MommaCis were great leaders of their families—which is the most important leadership context. Leadership development transpires when caretakers use camping, crabbing, fishing, and giving incremental responsibility—like going to the store alone—to teach children to deconstruct an event, and transform untangling fishing lines into life lessons that are being first introduced into the value systems of developing minds. These leadership fundamentals apply to every context, whether it is in a family or corporation, a religious or political institution, a playground or a board meeting.

Before starting any organization or attempting to do any work, leaders must craft a precise vision, mission, and value statement to create strategic plans to achieve organizational goals. Strategy without vision, mission, and values is dangerous because it is quite like getting behind the wheel of a car and driving while being blindfolded.

Think about it, would you get behind the wheel of your car and drive blindfolded to an unknown destination, without a reason, to do something you don't care about?

No? Yet executives get behind their desks daily to drive their organizations without vision, not having a targeted picture of where they're going, and without giving employees, customers, and communities reasons to care.

Without vision, people have no direction to follow. To lead is to give people a destination—so that you can influence behavior toward the goal of arriving at that destination.

Without mission, people have no purpose for following. To lead is to give people purpose—so that you can give them something bigger than themselves to believe in.

Without values, they have no guideposts for behavior. To lead is to establish values—so that you and your followers have expectations about behaviors and how you treat people and organizations.

Of everything I do as a consultant and coach, helping leaders craft vision, mission, and value statements is the hardest and most essential work to be done. It is hard because pinpointing where you want to go, how you want to get there, and the rules of conduct you must abide by is incredibly difficult to articulate in simple and convincing language. Drafting these statements must be done before even attempting to create strategic plans and goals because those plans must be tied to the vision, mission, and values. Organizations without vision, mission, and values, and the culture, teaching, and leadership to support them, will fail, and it will be the fault of leaders who don't know how to—or choose not to—create these statements. Apply these lessons wherever you lead—or you're not really leading at all.

# C = CONFLICT

## (HOW TO USE CONFLICT TO GENERATE WIN-WIN SOLUTIONS)

# 7

## WINNING CONFLICT

"I'm pregnant," said Mary, my grandmom, to her immigrant Roman Catholic Italian parents in 1946.

Grandmumpt snapped her head, glared with disbelief at her daughter, and shouted, "Whadda you mean youse-ah pregnant?"

"I'm sorry. It's true. I am pregnant. I know who the father is, but we're not together," said my grandmom.

"Jesus, Mary, and Joseph. You can't live with us anymore. Your father won't accept you. Neither will your brothers. This baby will bring shame to our family," said Grandmumpt.

Standard living arrangements for immigrant families imitated those back in the old country: daughters and sons stayed in their parents' house until they were married. While these living situations offered support that allowed children to grow into adults without the financial burdens of being kicked out of the house before they were "ready," the lack of privacy to create intimate relationships forced young lovers to find creative ways to spend romantic moments. Strict adherence to Catholic doctrine called for abstinence prior to marriage—a rule that if broken would condemn one's soul to eternal damnation—so we were told. Every Catholic knows this human-made rule; very few follow it. Even though Mary was in her early twenties, she still lived in her parents' home, waiting for a marriage proposal. But she didn't wait around like most folks, she went out and was active. In those days you didn't leave the house until you were married, and you certainly didn't engage in intimate acts prior to being married.

Family and religion are both institutions. All institutions have logics such as rules, value systems, cultural norms, history, structures, and belief systems that are path dependent. Path dependency theory begins with the premise the organizations and people participate in institutions that both provide structure and coerce behavioral standard and activities toward preexisting customary paths.[40] These paths were created either prior to the institution or after the institution by keepers of that institution whose purpose was to drive behavior and thought to perpetuate the institution. Choices about which path to take—or how to even decide on which path to take—are determined by prior choices that constrain the institution from developing and progressing. Effectively, history dictates the future. Once a path evolves, or is chosen, within an institution, the path itself becomes self-reinforcing and increasingly challenging to break free from. Over time, not following the path is known to institutional actors as dissonance, and the breaking of rules, values, and predetermined paths becomes punishable.

Mary broke the rules and got knocked up with her first child, out of wedlock, bringing shame down on her family. In the eyes of Grandmumpt, her daughter had broken the rules (no premarital intimacy), strayed from the path (get married, then move out), and violated the family or Catholic Church's values, punishable by excommunication from the family. Following the path of other "afflicted" Catholic families, traditions that cause pain of a bygone era, Grandmumpt and Great grandpop sent her to a nunnery. "You gonna move to the

Convent. The nuns will keep you there until you have the baby. You can't stay in dis house no more," said Grandmumpt. Mary would spend the next eight months in Philadelphia under the care of nuns. When she gave birth to her first child, Mary and her daughter Jeanie were ostracized from family. Split from familial support, Mary was forced into isolation, deep emotional despair, and loneliness.

"They abandoned me," Grandmom would later tell me. "When I needed my family most, they threw me away like a piece of trash. All in the name of their dignity, their belief that I was a sinner." Guilt is a part of life, and Mary was full of it. She became bitter, angry, and eventually disavowed her parents and siblings, all while raising my mother's older sister. Fighting became a family routine, immersing her generation in a path-dependent pattern of conflict that fostered awful psychosocial and familial outcomes.[41] On the off occasion that Mary did get together with family, she couldn't help herself from dredging up old grievances. Arguments inevitably escalated into shouting, crying, and storming out of houses with threats: "I'll never talk to you again. I hate this family." Over time these routines transformed into habitual patterns of behavior that disrupted our family relationships.

Eventually, conflict became the only path for Mary to take when in the presence of her family. Conflict became part of our family institution, it was an unwritten institutional logic— if with family then we must fight.

Mary was always the initiator of conflict. The only way Mary knew to relieve her pain was to pour it onto the people she blamed for causing it, including Mom and her sister Jeanie.

Grandmom grated on her own daughter relentlessly, letting Jeanie know that Jeanie was the cause of Grandmom's problems. In today's world, there's no doubt we would label this as emotional and psychological abuse. Back then, people simply said, "Mary's just hard on Jeanie."

Years of abusive language took its toll on Jeanie, as she suffered under constant conflict initiated by her own mother. To find peace outside a home full of conflict, Jeanie became conflict avoidant. "It's not worth the fight," Jeanie said. Mom and Grandmom would "Yell and scream all the time. I'd rather just not be there." And she wasn't. Jeanie avoided Mary, her sister/my mother, and us children at all costs. She also avoided conflict in every area—and with every other person—in her life. Whenever conflict arose, Jeanie would sink inside herself, going mentally back to the times when that timid little girl would be verbally abused by her mother. Come conflict in any degree and Jeanie would quit jobs, end romantic relationships, and exit platonic friendships. To Jeanie, every conflict, no matter how big or small, was a battle she chose not to fight.

Mom took the other route. Mom chose to be defensive, to stand her ground. Whenever Grandmom would fight with Mom, Mom would fight like hell right back, even as a little girl. Grandmom would lob over a grenade to Mom, "Don't be stupid!" Mom would reply, "Who you calling stupid?" Therein lay Grandmom's problem—she could not help but react to every situation in the only way she knew how—through escalating conflict. And, because of the effects of path dependency, driven by a family history of conflict, Mom could not help but react to Grandmom's reaction by escalating the conflict even further.

Boom.

Eruption.

Conflict escalation.

Cycle of conflict starts again.

Mom yells back, "Well, you raised me to be like this. So, I guess I shouldn't take parenting tips from you."

Now, instead of talking about the present conflict, they started name-calling and trading barbs. The original conflict now in the background, each one would shout insults and profanity, "*vaffanculo.*"

On days we'd visit Grandmom, the entire preamble of getting ready took an atomic nuclear toll on Mom. Fighting and mutually assured destruction were guaranteed outcomes any time mother and daughter were in the same room. Almost always, the screaming would start right after one, or both, took a verbal stab at the other. Predictably, their already delicate self-esteem would get bruised, historic slanders and barbs would be traded, and then one or the other of them would run from the room, crying, with their pinkies pushed together over the bridge of their nose in failed attempts to cover tear-stained faces.

Relentlessly attacking my concept of parent-child relationships, Grandmom and Mom shattered, from an early age, all perspective of what healthy loving parental relationships "look like" and should be. The mere mention of an impending visit would send me into a stress fit, causing me to bite my nails, and feel the nausea that comes with the anticipation of knowing two of the women I cared for the most, didn't care enough about me to at least pretend to have a loving relationship. There I was, in the middle, watching every fight with a first-row seat.

Two things came from watching those two women fight it out every time they were together.

First: What kind of parental relationship to *not* have with a child, how to not treat another person you purported to care about, how to experience pain-stress-anxiety-fear, and how to cause pain in the lives of children who watch their adult caretaker's fight. Watching them fight made me want to crawl inside my skin and scream. As a child, I vowed to never have a conflict filled relationship with my own children.

Second: How ridiculous it was to waste every second of time you have with a person by engaging in perpetual conflict. Really, why spend time with someone when the only thing that the two of you do is argue? It was a miserable way to pass an afternoon. Even as a child, I knew both were at fault for creating and sustaining conflict.

The pattern of leadership in a parent-child relationship starts with the parent being a leader of their children. Parenting is not about the parent, but rather about the parent taking care of themselves in a healthful way such that they can take care of their children in equally and more healthful ways. A parent who is not well emotionally, mentally, physically, spiritually, and yes, financially, is unable to devote their entire selves to their children. In the mind of an unhealthy parent, the ego, which is self-serving and self-protecting, tells the brain to dedicate all resources for recovery and recuperation to the self, leaving few resources available for nurturing the child. Consequently, the ego attacks anything that "takes away" from its own recovery, disabling the "giving" function that is compulsory for compassionate caregiving—even when that caregiving is for one's own progeny. Grandmom perceived Jeanie and Mom to be takers, and because she viewed her own child as the "problem," she was never able to extend herself lovingly toward her own daughters.

Grandmom and Mom's unhealthy relationship continued until the day my grandmother died, when, at thirteen years old, I was a freshman in high school. The only thing my mom ever knew was a lack of love and overt conflict. Walls were built around her heart to protect her from the hurt of not being loved, but she needed love more than anything else.

Although I loved her because she was my Grandmom, Mary's legacy is one of pain and suffering. Pain ruthlessly inflicted on Mom from the void in her heart that could never be filled. Suffering of her grandchildren though unhealthy relational patterns. Standing there, as a prepubescent teen at her wake, staring down at her cold dead body, smelling the formaldehyde seeping out of her decaying pores, I vowed never to be a parent like her. I swore to my God that my children would never be pained from the pain she caused in my life. I promised my unborn children, right at death's doorstep, that they would never suffer from my suffering.

At her funeral, on a rainy day that caused the dirt pile from the ditch that would become her home to turn into a mudslide, there was a picture of her standing next to Grandmumpt (her mother) and my mom (her daughter). It struck me how Grandmumpt, who was a leader of all people, could cause all this conflict by not accepting her daughter's pregnancy. Leaders fail, all the time.

I realized, as Grandmom's journey ended, amid an audience dressed in mourner's black, that every person must be responsible for their own journey of personal development. Because of the ferocity of the words I heard being flung from acid tongues, during spats of irate throw downs, I saw and felt the immediate impact of negative words, name-calling, and tyrannical parenting on the souls of its children. Realizing the wake of destruction Grandmom left, I suddenly felt relieved that she was gone. Her removal from earth triggered an unexpectedly deep retrieval of security; knowing that I would not have to bear witness to the viciousness of hurtful words and the whiplash of emotions. I learned from Grandmumpt how to be a central and powerful familial leader, and how one decision changed an entire family lineage. I learned from my

Grandmom how the effects of not giving love can screw up the well-being of multiple generations.

## DOOM LOOP

Defensiveness is a psychological mechanism with which we try to shield ourselves from danger, emotional-psychological-physical harm or threats, and embarrassment. Defensiveness anchors us in our instinctive protective behaviors, in this case physical confrontation as the expression of a hopelessly desperate mother. People who are on the defensive tend to become very good at doing what is not good for themselves, or good for anyone who crosses their path and stands the hair up on the back on their neck. Worst of all, defensiveness leads to what my conflict and negotiations professor calls a self-sealing, antilearning, *doom loop*.

The doom loop started when Mom would say one thing and do another.

Between the laughing and crying, Mom and Grandmom would both deny, or pretend they were unaware, of the root of the problem. They'd ask each other "what's wrong?" and lie when saying "nothing," both knowing they were incapable of talking in a controlled manner. These denials themselves prohibited learning. No progress was ever made toward resolving the conflict because neither person wanted to do the hard relational and emotional work to solve the problem, to do the hard work of being honest with one another, to dig in and tell the truth about their mistakes, addictions, and weaknesses.

Making matters worse, the moment Mom and Grandmom denied to one another that anything was broken in their own individual life—and by extension their relationship—they simply moved on to discussing other topics as if the entire cracked reality that we existed in was a normal, healthy condition. Our life was not healthy. By all measures it was a house of alcoholism, violence, and dysfunctional adult relationships that caused deep trauma in them and in my sister and me.

Denying reality made the denial itself not discussable. Not discussing the denial itself became not discussable. The denial itself isn't being discussed, and the fact that we aren't discussing the denial—as though the denial itself isn't a thing that exists and continues to perpetuate conflict—isn't something even that can be discussed unto itself.

At this point in any conflict, people don't discuss why they get so angry because no one wants to address the larger issues affecting the relationship and situation. The resultant noncommunicative hamster wheel perpetuated because, in their words, alcoholism, infidelity, spousal abuse are "things we just don't talk about," creating in their minds the fiction that the conflict was over.

Conflict is dynamic like water and will flow into whatever opening is available. Just as the waves of seawater will predictably grow when whipped by the frenzy of wind above or volcanic eruption below, conflict will grow when overt disagreement occurs from above or when simmering resentment is harbored below the surface of words and behaviors. In the mind of the deniers, conflict is over when shouting, abusing, and fighting temporarily abate. Incorrectly assuming resolution has been made, all learning stops in a conflict. Having neither the maturity, will, or skills to navigate conflict, Mom and Grandmom stuck us kids in a doom loop of Groundhog Day from hell.

Research has shown that our approach to conflict isn't solely determined by our upbringing. There's a biological component too. Studies in behavioral genetics have demonstrated that certain personality traits, including those related to conflict resolution, have a heritable component.[42] This interplay between nature and nurture shapes our predisposition to conflict and our methods of addressing it.

The neurological effects of such chronic conflict and trauma are profound and far-reaching. Research has shown that exposure to persistent conflict and violence can lead to changes in brain structure and function, particularly in areas related to stress response and emotional regulation.[43] The constant activation of the body's stress response system leads to elevated levels of cortisol and other stress hormones, which can impair cognitive function, decision-making abilities, and even physical health.

In our family, this constant state of conflict likely contributed to a cycle of stress and poor decision-making that perpetuated our dysfunctional dynamics. It's a pattern that I've seen replicated in many organizational settings, where chronic conflict creates a toxic environment that affects not just the immediate parties involved, but the entire system.

## WHY YOU SHOULD CARE ABOUT CONFLICT WITHIN ORGANIZATIONS, TEAMS, AND EMPLOYEE RELATIONSHIPS

This deeply personal history of familial conflict isn't just a story of individual struggles; it mirrors the complex dynamics of conflict that play out in organizations every day. Just as our family's conflicts were shaped by cultural norms, personal histories, institutional logics, and path-dependent patterns of response retaliation, organizational conflicts are influenced by similar forces. Conflict patterns in organizations often emerge from historical events, cultural norms, and established power structures. Over time, these patterns become ingrained in the organizational culture, creating a self-reinforcing cycle that can be difficult to break.

Path dependency in conflict resolution means that the way an organization has dealt with conflicts in the past heavily influences how it will approach conflicts in the future. Leaders need to understand their existing organization's conflict patterns. Is there a culture of avoidance where issues are swept under the rug? Or is there a more combative culture where disagreements quickly escalate into personal attacks? Does the organization have a history of top-down decision-making where employees are accustomed to not voicing their opinions, leading to suppressed task conflicts that could have led to better outcomes? If an organization has always resolved conflicts through authoritarian measures, it creates a path that makes it difficult to implement more collaborative conflict resolution methods later. These patterns become institutionalized, with new employees learning to conform to this conflict pattern.

Leaders can break these institutional patterns, where constructive conflict is encouraged and destructive conflict is minimized, by doing the following:

- *Create Psychological Safety*: Team members need to feel safe expressing disagreement without fear of retribution.

- *Encourage Healthy Debate*: Make it clear that respectful disagreement is welcome and can lead to better outcomes.

- *Model Good Conflict Resolution Behaviors*: Leaders should demonstrate how to disagree respectfully and work toward mutually beneficial solutions.

- *Provide Conflict Resolution Training*: Equip employees with the skills to handle conflict effectively.

- *Address Conflicts Promptly*: Don't let issues fester. Address them early before they escalate.

- *Use Conflict As A Learning Opportunity*: After resolving a conflict, reflect on what can be learned from the experience.

Learning about what drives any given conflict is essential to solving that conflict. Studies about integrating people and organizations indicate that the most opportune time for conflict is when organizations engage in some form of change process.[44] Change creates opportunities for conflict because change involves breaking known patterns of work and behavior, providing the opportunity to learn something new. Too often leaders impose change without considering the effects of those changes on workers' routines, lives, and career aspirations. When this happens, the leader dictates change and transmits information in a single direction—from leader to follower. Single-loop learning centers around a person or entity singularly imposing its will on others, by engaging in behavioral modifications that seek only unidirectional instruction. Single-loop learning creates path-dependent reinforcement of existing policies while simultaneously creating dysfunctional resistance response patterns to healthy and productive change efforts.

Double-loop learning refers to the questioning of basic assumptions held by both parties intertwined in conflict, seeking understanding of the fundamental issues at hand. Double-loop learning is powerful because it involves the challenging of one's own beliefs and proactively seeking constant changing of behavior to produce desirable outcomes. To win at conflict is to ensure that all parties share in a win-win solution. A powerful way to create win-win solutions is to apply the principles of double-loop learning, to understand the root of the conflict, the path-dependent causes of the conflict, and the opportunities for growth-oriented, mutually beneficial solutions that arise from the many different types of conflict.

In organizations, conflict manifests in various types, each with its own challenges and potential benefits.[45, 46]

- *Task Conflict*: This involves disagreements about the content and outcomes of work. It is the most common type of conflict in organizations and often arises from differences in viewpoints, ideas, or opinions about how to accomplish specific goals or tasks. When managed properly, task conflict can lead to improved decision-making and innovation. Leaders should encourage healthy debate around tasks and projects, as it can lead to better outcomes. For example, in a marketing team, one person argues for a social-media focused campaign for their new smartphone, while the other insists on prioritizing traditional TV advertisements.

- *Process Conflict*: These are disagreements about methods, procedures, or resources used to complete tasks. For example, during software development, the front-end team wants to use React for building the user interface, but the back-end team insists on using a full-stack framework like Django to streamline the entire development process. On the positive side, process conflicts can highlight inefficiencies, spark innovation, and lead to clearer guidelines when addressed constructively. It is best to solve process conflict early in team formation and at the start of projects. Left unmanaged, process conflict leads to dysfunctional and inefficient work patterns that increase employee frustration and turnover. Effective leaders must proactively manage process conflicts by establishing clear procedures, encouraging open communication, and being receptive to feedback and improvements.

- *Role Conflict*: Unclear or conflicting job expectations lead to stress and decreased job satisfaction. Clear job descriptions and regular communication mitigate role conflict. An example: a project manager feels caught between the demands of upper management and the needs of their team, leading to role conflict that needs to be addressed through clear communication and potentially restructuring responsibilities.

- *Cognitive Conflict*: This entails disagreements over the best decision based on competing information or opposing critiques of the same information. It occurs when team members have different interpretations of data or prioritize different factors in decision making. Leaders should encourage open discussion of diverse perspectives and facilitate evidence-based decision-making to resolve cognitive conflict. For example, when two scientists disagree on the interpretation of research findings, cognitive conflict can lead to a deeper exploration of the data and a more robust conclusion.

- *Pseudoconflict*: This is a misunderstanding that occurs when individuals believe they know what the other person is thinking but are inaccurate in their assumptions. Pseudoconflict can escalate quickly if not addressed, as misinterpretations can lead to hurt feelings and resentment. An example might be when a team member misinterprets a colleague's email as critical, leading to pseudoconflict that can be resolved through a simple conversation. Active listening, clarification, and open communication are essential to resolve pseudoconflict.

- *Ego Conflict*: Ego conflict is an emotional dislike for another person that often results from a worsening of pseudoconflict. Triggered by defensiveness and emotional responses, it is characterized by personal attacks, defensiveness, and a focus on winning rather than finding solutions. An example might be when two team members have a personality clash that escalates into personal attacks and undermines collaboration. Ego conflict is highly destructive and can quickly poison a work environment. Leaders need to intervene promptly to mediate ego conflicts, encourage empathy and understanding, and refocus the team on shared goals.

- *Intragroup Conflict*: Perceived incompatibilities or differences among group members comprise intragroup conflict. It is marked by disagreements about tasks, processes, roles, or interpersonal relationships within the team. Intragroup conflict is constructive when done in the spirit of healthy competition that drives productivity, and destructive when competition threatens the jobs, status, reputation, and promotability of losing group members. Leaders need to foster a culture of open communication, respect, and collaboration to ensure that intragroup conflict leads to positive outcomes. For instance, when team members have different working styles, intragroup conflict can arise, but it can also lead to a more diverse and creative approach to problem-solving.

- *Intergroup Conflict*: Intergroup conflict entails perceived incompatibilities or differences between groups. It can involve competition for resources, status, or recognition, as well as differences in goals, values, or cultures. An example might be when two departments within a company compete for budget allocations, leading to intergroup conflict that needs to be addressed through negotiation and compromise. Intergroup conflict can be highly destructive and can lead to decreased productivity, low morale, and even sabotage. Leaders need to promote intergroup cooperation, encourage understanding and appreciation of different perspectives, and foster a shared sense of purpose to mitigate intergroup conflict.

## THOMAS-KILMANN CONFLICT MODE INSTRUMENT—
## FIVE CONFLICT-HANDLING STYLES

The Thomas-Kilmann Conflict Mode Instrument (TKI) is a widely recognized model that identifies five primary styles individuals use when handling conflict.[47] These styles are:

- *Competing*: This is marked by high assertiveness and low cooperativeness. This style aims to win at the expense of the other party. It can be useful in emergencies or when quick, decisive action is needed, but overuse can lead to resentment and damaged relationships.

- *Collaborating*: This style is typified by high assertiveness and high cooperativeness. This style aims to find a solution that fully satisfies both parties. It is ideal for complex issues where creative solutions are needed, but it can be time-consuming.

- *Compromising*: Moderate assertiveness and moderate cooperativeness are hallmarks of the compromising style. This style aims to find a mutually acceptable solution that partially satisfies both parties. It is useful when time is limited or when a temporary solution is needed.

- *Accommodating*: This entails low assertiveness and high cooperativeness. This style involves giving in to the other party's wishes. It can be appropriate when preserving harmony is more important than winning, but overuse can lead to resentment and lack of influence.

- *Avoiding*: Low assertiveness and low cooperativeness. This style involves sidestepping the conflict. It can be useful for trivial issues or when more important matters need attention, but overuse can lead to unresolved problems and missed opportunities.

To effectively apply the TKI in leadership, consider the following detailed approach:

- Self And Team Assessment:
  - Identify your and your team members' default conflict style through observation, self-reflection, or by taking the TKI assessment.
  - Analyze past conflict situations to recognize patterns in your behavior.
  - Understand the strengths and limitations of your and their preferred styles.
- Conflict Style Workshops:
  - Organize team training sessions on the TKI model.
  - Conduct role-playing exercises to practice different conflict styles.
  - Discuss real-world scenarios and how different styles could be applied.
- Situational Adaptability:
  - Learn to recognize when each conflict style is most appropriate.
  - Develop the flexibility to switch between styles as needed.

- Regularly review and discuss conflict situations with your team.
- Conflict Style Matching:
  - When mediating conflicts, consider the styles of those involved.
  - Adapt your approach to bridge gaps between conflicting parties.
  - Encourage team members to recognize and adapt to others' styles.

Navigating conflict is indeed an essential skill that few people work on, yet it is crucial for organizational success. Conflict exists everywhere in organizations, from strategic disagreements in the boardroom to interpersonal squabbles between coworkers. Use these recommended approaches to minimize destructive conflicts and harness the power of diverse perspectives to drive innovation and foster a more engaged, collaborative work environment.

# L = LEARNING

## (HOW TO BE A MENTOR
## AND LEARN EVERY DAY)

# 8

# MILLION-DOLLAR
# LIFE-CHANGING DECISIONS

The grand commune of Fontainebleau is located southeast of Paris. From its inception as a hamlet circa AD 1137, the "fountain of the forest" has enchanted everyone from peasants and popes to monarchs and the masses. Fontainebleau is also home to INSEAD University, Europe's most prestigious business school. INSEAD is the Harvard of Europe. The world-famous professors and practitioners who comprise its faculty have put together a world-class program, Continuing Education and Development for Executives and Professionals (CEDEP). Designed to be an elite "training ground," CEDEP allows companies to send groups of high-potential employees to INSEAD for an eighteen-month graduate-level advanced business leadership curriculum.

"The British are coming," said the company gossip, quoting the famed saying that, as legend has it, was shouted by Paul Revere as he bravely rode his horse from city to city warning of the impending British invasion of the American colonies. "It's a hostile takeover. We're gonna lose our jobs if they buy us." StudentCity was a privately owned and operated tourism business based in Peabody, Massachusetts. Local folks with generations of family who could trace their lineage back to the original settlers were wary of any hint of British incursions.

First Choice (FC) is a United Kingdom-based conglomerate specializing in niche, experienced-based travel and holidays. FC meant to use StudentCity as a launching pad to break into the North American leisure tourism industry. StudentCity was a perfect fit: a student-market tour operator specializing in spring break for college students and summer break educational tours for high school students. FC would need a deep bench of talented leaders, with a succession plan and promotional trajectory for its leadership team and the owners of the companies it acquired.

Weeks after StudentCity was acquired, Maurizio, the CEO, pulled me into his office. "You and two other leaders have been selected for CEDEP. You'll be going to INSEAD and to the corporate headquarters in London. You'll be the first American trio to join over twenty other leaders. These other leaders represent as many companies as they do countries of origin. Your peers from other countries will form a cohort. Welcome to the big time. Buckle up. The ride from here on will be fast, challenging, and, whether we like it or not, more corporate."

FC rightly chose to develop leaders from within its ranks, acculturating and training them from newly acquired companies, through an immersive international educational experience. That was smart on its behalf because the connections and alliances formed by newly acquired leaders strengthened the interconnectivity of a global brand, creating opportunities for collaboration and problem-solving among executives around the world.

The first time I stepped foot onto the INSEAD campus, my mind exploded with possibilities. Years had passed since my derriere graced the seat of a school desk. Without understanding what had been lacking before sitting in the raised auditorium seating, I could feel myself becoming more complete. I missed school, and INSEAD was the "Business School for the World." Here I was, a kid from the streets of New Castle, Delaware, now walking inside an elite world-class university, moments after strolling along some of Europe's most historically significant promenades.

I went back and forth across "the pond," the cheeky term Brits use to label the Atlantic Ocean, to Fontainebleau and London, spending time in ornately decorated palaces and classrooms where many of the world's top companies sent their leaders. Our cohort of developing leaders was made of Americans, British, Egyptians, Greeks, Turks, and others from a globally dispersed set of formerly privately held companies now tasked to lead their own brands within a publicly traded globally dispersed organization. During lecture, discussion, and group work, professors revealed best practices and practical, strategic planning tools, marketing plans, and, most importantly to corporations, how to drive value for stockholders. Eyes wide open, I stared headlong into a future I couldn't possibly have imagined without being exposed to the highest level of executive education, cultural infusion, and brilliant thinkers present in our cohort.

"This is all great," said Divok, the Turk. "We're learning as leaders of our business. But what about our employees? We can't send every employee to INSEAD. So how do we train them?"

Divok was speaking to our professor of human resources, who answered, "No, it's cost prohibitive to send all employees to a program like CEDEP. Leaders are the ones who make decisions about how to train their people. Everyone in this room is a leader of their company. It's up to you to figure out how to spend your money on training and development—how much money, and on what training and development, consultants, retreats, and speakers you choose to focus on. Ask yourself, "What do I want from my team? What is the ROI for every dollar spent on developing leaders in my organization?" Then, figure out how to pay for the training that will get you the desired results."

Prior to hearing those statements, I hadn't considered that all employees, not just executives and managers, should be trained, developed, and given opportunities to lead in their work roles. It never occurred to me to train employees on leading rather than just training them to do their jobs effectively. *What can I do? How can I change the system? What does training and development look like for my employees?*

For years, I did what came naturally to me, using my charisma and extroversion to lead people and build relationships, intuition to make decisions, and linear thinking for planning and logistics. Turns out I could be a mostly effective manager by using life experiences from sports, church, and getting my ass kicked from the time I was born. Combine some knowledge from my economics undergraduate degree and years spent watching leaders, and voilà, I'm a person in charge of a $27 million budget, ten full-time salespeople, thousands of part-time salespeople, and an entire destination and program in Acapulco, where I negotiated all contracts with hotels and vendors *en Español*. I also became the corporate trainer, flying to destinations such as Jamaica, Cancún, Punta Cana, Puerto Vallarta, and Mazatlán to train American and local staff. And I did it all without ever having read a single word on how to become an effective leader.

All that time, I wrote the sales manual, designed the training goals, created the agenda, and was the speaker/trainer for all the events. Over time, my formula was perfected, and our sales grew by double digits annually. Success was largely attributed to the effectiveness of these trainings. Ultimately, I'd put together a bunch of slides that mirrored the pages in the manual. Lecturing nonstop and talking incessantly for eight hours per day, my approach to teaching was routed in the traditions I'd grown up learning: a know-it-all teacher/professor/trainer illuminating an audience of gawking onlookers sitting on the edge of their seats, hanging on every word the oracle was graciously blessing their ears with. I was an amazing trainer—or so I thought. (I'd later learn—on the first day of the first class on the first page of the first book assigned for reading in my doctoral program—that lecturing is among the least effective ways to train adults! Bam. In da face. Another crushing blow to my leader identity.)

It became abundantly clear that I was leading by gut instinct, making it up as I went along. Gone was my interest in managing, and what awakened in me was an unquenchable thirst for knowledge and self-actualization. INSEAD taught me many things, none more important than this: Stop leading from your gut.

CEDEP was realistically an MBA program without the culminating acknowledgment on paper of having earned a formal degree from INSEAD. I was thirsty for knowledge and hungry for new information on how to be a better manager and leader. The local library and the Barnes & Noble section on management and personal improvement became new favorite haunts. Having no idea what I was looking for, except to improve my performance and satiate my ambition to advance, I bought and consumed books like *Good to Great* (Jim Collins), *Emotional Intelligence* (Daniel Goleman), and other lesser-known practical workbooks.[48][49] The more I read, the more I knew I didn't know enough. How could I be so ignorant of such topics?

Of all the things in the world of people in organizations, what fascinates me most is figuring out how to improve employees' performance while simultaneously improving the quality of their lives. Former CEOs, researchers, scholars, management consultants, and other experts attest to organizations' absolute responsibility to develop talent within their workforce because longer-term training programs improve employee performance, increase engagement, reduce turnover, create efficiencies, and help identify new markets—all things that increase revenue and profitability.

> *When companies invest in employees, they'll work harder, smarter, and more efficiently; be less likely to quit and more likely to stay; and form bonds with the company when leaders care about people. Study after study shows that people who learn to lead better have employees who work harder, produce more work, make fewer errors, attract more and higher paying clients, lose fewer clients, have greater satisfaction at work, and contribute to a positive culture.*

Questions about developing leaders are the foundation of my boundless search for becoming a better leader, manager, and human being. *What can we learn about ROI from training leaders? What can we learn about strategically developing our workforce? How will investments in training (employees) lead to more sales and revenue? How can our human resource development initiatives better the quality of life for employees? Is there a company I can hire to train my leaders—a company that specializes in training leaders? A company specializing in developing executives,* managers, and employees can do a better job than my internal staff—but finding one of those is like finding a unicorn.

> For the record, there isn't a more certain way to double your money than to invest in your employees to develop them as leaders. Peer-reviewed research found that, on average, the range of ROI "exceeds 200% for longer term interventions depending on location and level of participant in the program."[50]

To calculate ROI, compare the net savings (cost savings minus the investment in leadership development) with the initial investment. For example, if your organization invested $100,000 in leadership development and you expect $300,000 in additional operating profit, the expected ROI is 200 percent.

## ROI On Leader Development Formula = (Net Gain from Investment - Initial Investment)/ Initial Investment

People who perform better produce more and make fewer errors—leading to cost avoidance and creating more revenue for the company. Add to the equation that people who are trained by their company and given a path for career advancement are likely to stay longer, less likely to quit, and more likely to add value to the organization—it's pretty easy to see that companies who want to grow need to spend a little bit of money to get a whole lot of benefit and revenue from the employees they train.

Having made this conclusion based on good science and seeing this very concept play out in my own experience, I decided to continue my education by getting an MBA. The purpose was to figure out how the best companies, scholars, and consultants were developing leaders. MBA programs taught the "how-to" of management, giving students a "tool kit" to take with them into future and more powerful leadership roles. When you get an MBA, your plan is to get promoted at your current organization—or get another job at a higher rank and pay—and be a high-level executive who leads their organization.

Months into the MBA, I realized that I was learning tools, but didn't understand the why, to what degree, under what conditions, how much is enough and how little makes too little a difference, and everything else behind how these "how-to tool kits" were supposed to work. It was not enough for me to know that I had the tools, as any MBA student would; I needed to understand the genesis of the tools, the research behind them, and how to create new tools and leadership training programs.

Halfway through my MBA program, Kristen asked the million-dollar question, "How long do you see yourself in the tourism and hospitality business? What will you do with your life, knowing the MBA doesn't give you the wisdom, knowledge, and power you crave to improve your life and leadership? You're going to go get a PhD."

"What? How in the world did you know that I was going to say that?"

Kristen said, "It is obvious that you are not satisfied with the MBA. You will not feel complete until you have finished this journey until its logical conclusion, to become a doctor. You are clearly miserable at work. The MBA is not preparing you for anything other than more corporate jobs, which you don't want. Money isn't your motivation, learning is. Put all that together and it just means more learning for you. Ultimately, you want to control your own future, and our future as a couple. You can't do that in your current job."

"You do know what that means right?" I did the math. "The immediate financial consequences of resigning from my job merit thoughtful consideration. I could continue to make $120K annual salary, plus commissions, bonuses, and other earn out opportunities—and don't forget tuition reimbursement, which would eliminate $80K in student debt from my MBA program. Over the course of the six years it would take me from application to graduation of a PhD program, I would have earned somewhere close to $1M. Or I might make $18K a year as a doctoral student and research assistant, earning a grand total of $72K over four years as a student in the program. Let's see, what else to consider...relocating and associated costs, there's the 80 percent dropout rate of PhD students. The uncertainty of finding a professor's job post-graduation coupled with the certainty, if fortunate to find a job, of relocating yet again. And, the real estate market and entire economy just collapsed, meaning that my real estate holdings are now worth about one-third of their former value. I'll be without a job, in a rental market where my student stipend does not cover half the monthly rent costs."

"I know. I'll get a job and pay the bills while you go to school. Your job will be school. We can do it, together. You'll see. It'll be fine," she said.

It was because of moments like these, where Kristen led me to understand myself better, and how she was always the light uncovering the best hidden parts of myself, that I had made life-changing *Decision #1: Marry Kristen.* She was and is my best friend and partner in life. I knew she was the one the first moment I laid eyes on her; twenty years of union later we have two kids, two businesses, and one great marriage.

Kristen had gently led me to *Decision #2: Quit my job and become a PhD.* I had self-discovered my path, was prepared to bet again on myself—along with Kristen's love and support—and planned to play the long game.

> *To become my future best self, I needed to break completely free from the shackles of my then current self. To become the me that was the fullest expression of me, I had to kill the version of myself that I no longer wanted to be.*

Resolved to my decision, I offered to the three C's—Maurizio, Jacques, and Patrick—an autobiographical account of my self-discovery journey, expressing along the way a fervent desire for continued self-improvement. Then, I resigned on good terms.

A few weeks later: Ring. Ring. Ring. Jacques, the COO who had recruited and then said goodbye to me when I resigned—the same creative genius who literally created the MTV Spring Break event stage that would popularize the phenomenon for the next twenty years—was calling.

"Hello."

Jacques said, "I have some good news to share. StudentCity is going to be the featured company on the next season of *The Real World.* Each season the cast works together at a job. Bunim Murray (the production company that created *The Real World* television show) is going to film and produce the cast working as staff members for the Cancún program in 2009. How exciting is that?"

"OMG. That is amazing. Congratulations. You should be very proud. Good for the business."

"There is an opportunity for you, Bryan," said Jacques. "The show needs to cast a boss. I want you to be the boss. You'll have to go onsite for the spring break season. You'll be the destination director, just like you were in Acapulco, only this time, you'll be leading the Cancún program. You'll do the corporate training, just like you've done in the past. I need you."

"Wow! This is great Jacques. Thank you for considering me. What's the catch?"

"So, you'll do it? It has got to be you. You are the highest-level person we know that will serve the brand properly and be a good onscreen leader. I believe in you."

As a rule, I never turn down offers on the first go around. This though, was a Michael Corleone moment: "Just when I thought I was out, they pull me back in."

"I have to consider it more."

"Will you at least take a call with the show's executives?"

"Sure. When?"

Two days later: Ring. Ring.

"Hello."

"Hi, Bryan. So, I hear that you're going to be our next star boss," said the determined voice on the other end of the phone call, an executive from the show.

*Decision #3, I am grateful for the offer. I must decline.* "I know how much this project means to Jacques, and StudentCity, but I am not your guy. My path is to become a professor and speaker. My PhD program begins six months after filming, which means the first episodes will come out just as I am sitting for my first classes."

The show's executive said, "I hear ya. Think about it though. This could be your big break. You could become famous. Some of the cast go on to have successful careers in the entertainment industry. Plus, if you want to become a speaker, this will give your name brand recognition."

All that was being said had occurred to me, and been given great contemplation, prior to hearing them articulate it to me so persuasively. Yes, I knew that being on the show would bring name recognition and pseudo celebrity status. During my time working in tourism and hospitality, I had met many *Real World* cast members, actors, singers, rappers, and celebrities of all sorts. Almost all of them had one thing in common...they really enjoyed being in the entertainment business and wanted fame and fortune that accompanied celebrity. I, on the other hand, wanted none of those things. I had chosen a path, a very difficult path, but it was my path. It was not glorious or showy, and certainly not destined for fame or fortune. Kristen and I were engaged to be married by the time this call was taking place, and above all else, to submit to another season of spring break, MTV *Real World* or not, would have been a selfish endeavor of pure vanity sure to sow disharmony in our upcoming nuptials. This line of reasoning, though, was almost unfathomable to my suitor, on account of most people he encountered having want of the spoils of celebrity he so richly promised.

"Bryan, c'mon, you gotta realize the potential in this. This is a launching pad. From everything I hear, you are the guy for this spot. You must do it," the executive said.

I didn't "must do it." On the contrary, because I had spent the better part of a year getting to know who I was, who I wanted to become, and with whom I wanted to spend the rest of my life, my conviction to stay on my chosen path was unwavering. No amount of discussion or persuasion could sway me away from the path. No enticements or compensation would deter me from marrying the women of my dreams and giving her the life we had divined after years of hard work on our relationship. I knew the future, and it was everlasting. Much longer than fifteen minutes of fame ever would have given.

MommaCis had taught me to pivot and be decisive. I had decided to pivot away from spring break and toward becoming a PhD. Decided. Done. Forward, not reverse. Over the course of my life, no lesson has had a more utilitarian and practical application. When you feel something tingling in the back of your brain, an unknown and indescribable unsettledness that crawls at you during you most silent times of solitude, that something is your next calling. Who is doing the calling, you ask? Your future best self is. The best version of you is in its embryonic form, giving you reason to raise it from infancy to adulthood, thriving at each stage along the way. Your path will become clear with introspective self-discovery.

Four years would pass between my first steps in Fontainebleau, France, and my first steps on the Boca Raton, Florida, campus of Florida Atlantic University for PhD courses. During those times, I had a rough-and-tumble battle royal between my own ears. Years thirty to thirty-four of my life would be among the most transformative. I could not label or identify where I was going—until I could. Once I had discerned and prayed upon my future, I pivoted without fear, choosing a new path, death of an old life, and taking decisive actions to manifest a vision of my future best self that required rebirth. Along the way, I made decisions to apply and be accepted into an MBA and subsequently a PhD program, resign from a promising career and sacrifice nearly $1 million in compensation, and turn down an offer to appear in a television show.

To make those types of monumental decisions you must come to know yourself, and what you want to become. Then, sacrifice in the short run everything you have ever worked for to ensure that you will sacrifice less in the long run.

In my life, I had made it from picking up free lunches from the backs of government funded food assistance programs to the halls of famed castles and world-class educational institutions. Now, I was on my way to the ivory tower; a tower no doubt comparable in stature to the castle so gorgeously gracing the village of Fontainebleau.

True leaders must decide their path and commit to it, no matter the costs. Life is about learning, and real leaders equip themselves with knowledge that changes the game for themselves and others. You must learn to lead, and that's what I did, and it changed my life—and it can change yours too.

My journey from the streets to the halls of INSEAD and beyond is a testament to the power of education and self-discovery in leadership. It's not just about acquiring tools or techniques; it's about fundamentally transforming yourself and your understanding of what leadership means.

> *The path to becoming a true leader is not always glamorous or lucrative in the short term. It often requires sacrifices and difficult decisions. But the long-term rewards—both personal and professional—are immeasurable.*

Learning to lead is a continuous process. It involves constant self-reflection, a willingness to challenge your assumptions, and the courage to step out of your comfort zone. It's about recognizing that true leadership is not about wielding power, but about empowering others and creating value for your organization and society at large.

By committing to this path of continuous learning and self-improvement, you open up possibilities not just for yourself, but for everyone you lead. You become a catalyst for positive change, capable of transforming organizations and lives.

Remember, the journey of leadership is not about reaching a destination; it's about who you become along the way. Embrace the challenges, seek out knowledge, and never stop striving to be your best self. That's how you become a leader worth following, and that's how you create lasting impact in the world.

# 9

# BE A MENTOR; CHANGE A LIFE

To learn is to teach. To become a better leader yourself, be a mentor. Approximately 70 percent of Fortune 500 companies employ mentoring programs as a form of human resource development,[51] and scholars suggest everyone, from CEOs to first-line employees, needs a mentor.[52]

A mentor at work is typically described as a significant figure within your professional contexts, possessing extensive expertise and experience, dedicated to fostering career growth and offering guidance in your professional journey.[53]

Mentorships have been described as a relationship between a more experienced person (mentor) who provides career and psychosocial support to a less experienced person (protégé) within an organization.[54] People want uncomplicated exchanges from anyone who provides small bits of "developmental input" to improve their performance.

Career support includes giving challenging assignments to a protégé, job coaching, protection and preservation, career strategizing, information sharing, augmenting positive exposure to executives, and sponsoring the protégé for promotions.

Psychosocial support involves providing emotional support, friendship, role modeling, inspiration and motivation, acceptance and confirmation, counseling, and personal feedback.[55]

Mentors and protégés seek developmental relationships

wherein both people teach and learn—relationships characterized by reciprocity, reward, and synergy. In its optimal form, development becomes synergistic comentoring, "a dyadic, synergistic, developmental relationship, in which mutually supportive co-mentors collaborate as an enduring unit to accomplish collective goals."[56]

Developmental relationships are interdependent, complex, and vitally important to developers' and learners' career success.[57] Faced with ambiguous and multidirectional career trajectories, particularly in uncertain environments in which changes in occupation and organizations are common, such as pandemics, economic recession, and the Great Resignation, individuals have become increasingly responsible for self-development.[58] Workers are now likely to cobble together a network of developers, what I label a 360° support circle.

A 360° support circle is a person's egocentric and dynamic constellation of mentors from personal nonwork contexts (e.g., educational, familial, community) and work contexts (e.g., associations, jobs, boards), who offer personal and professional development.[59] It's a developmental network comprised of all the people you can seek help from when needed and those who offer help when able—and you use their help to advance your life and leadership. Some of your mentors you'll easily identify, while others will be strangers who cross your path for a fleeting moment to affect you in mysteriously profound ways. Often, the usual suspects are helpers: parents, caretakers, and friends. Other times, help comes from unknown people in unforeseeable circumstances: civil servants, paramedics, people who believe in your vision and cause, and communities that support their neighbors. Help comes from teachers, professors, executive coaches, authors, trainers, speakers, TED Talk presenters, living and dead people who live/lived a model life you strive to emulate—such that their life motivates you to improve your own, experts who know more than you about a specific topic, and mentors who guide you on an array of personal and professional areas.[60]

The rest of this chapter introduces you to some of my mentors who helped me achieve my life's goals. Their impact on my life is positive and powerful. If it weren't for their dedication to helping others and offering themselves as mentors, I wouldn't have climbed the mountains that made me who I am today.

## FIGURING OUT HOW TO CLIMB MOUNTAINS

The Marble Mountains in Da Nang, Vietnam, is a cluster of five separate mountains and home to a Buddhist monastery. Ngu Hanh Son, or Five Elements Mountain, as it is known in Vietnamese, is named after what the Asian philosophy consider each of the universe's five basic elements of life: metal, water, air, fire, plant, and soil. Marble Mountains sit across from miles-long sweeping views of China Beach (My Khe Beach) and An Bang Beach where, during the Vietnam War, American soldiers like Daddy Tommy would sojourn for rest, recuperation, and indulgence in the allures of local grass. Atop Thuy Son (Water Mountain) sits Tam Thai Pagoda, where monks take residence and farm the pasture of open fields that give way to the Huyen Khong cave, where sits a hand carved three-yard-high Buddha. Buddha watches over everyone and everything, including generations of past revolutionaries and war planners who used Huyen Khong cave as a secret hideout for military strategizing and providing treatment to wounded and dead soldiers.

My MBA program included an educational trip to Vietnam,

where we would tour capitalistic businesses and industries in a Communist country. Our itinerary would take us across Vietnam to Ho Chi Minh City (Saigon), Da Nang, Hoi An, and Hanoi.

As I looked down from atop of Marble Mountain, I tried to envision the previous carnage of bodies and blood that covered the same beach that was now, in contrast, dotted with bikinis and sunbathers caressing pebbles of sand in front of crashing ocean waves. How different the world is now from when the forbearers of present-day monks carried dead and wounded soldiers from sea level up 165 stone stairs to the monastery where medical stations were hidden deep within caves. With herculean strength monks carried soldiers up the sides of mountains on handmade gurneys that made the trek to the top both treacherous and almost humanly impossible. I looked down at those steps and the impossible feat that the monks accomplished and thought about the challenges that I would face getting into and completing a PhD program.

The journey to become a doctor was a destiny that I had no idea where it would begin or how it would end, and somehow in that moment, seemed as impossible as carrying deadweight up the side of a mountain. There I was atop Thuy Son Mountain, having an epiphany while surrounded by uncomplicated people (monks) who lived a simple life with purpose. The monks' ambition was to serve humanity and yet my ambition was to serve my ambition of perpetual climb. I acknowledged my admiration of people who choose to live uncomplicated lives while I simultaneously pontificated on ways to further complicate my own life—by pursuing a PhD—during an already complicated MBA program, all the while trying to figure out my life's purpose.

At the bottom of a perilous descent is a gift shop, and in that gift shop are the works of monks who spend their days and nights carving away on marble so that people with less virtuous lives can leave with souvenirs. A beautiful marble chessboard with handcrafted pieces sat gorgeously on a white counter. I thought to myself, *what a complicated gift to get back to America and yet I feel compelled to purchase it. Kristen will love it. All trip long you've been looking for something meaningful to bring back, to memorialize that you were thinking of her on this trip.*

Years before, Kristen had taught me how to play chess, mentoring me on the rules and strategies. Kristen said, "In chess, you must plan many moves ahead; sometimes, you must plan to make small sacrifices to make big gains." As I learned the game of chess at her side, we pontificated on life. Chess is a metaphor for life, and life is a game of chess. It dawned on me that the entire strategy of getting into a PhD program should be played like a game of chess.

All students must write a thesis as part of the MBA gradu-ation requirements. I had a brilliant idea on how to economize my time completing my thesis and achieve my goal of getting into a PhD program. I approached my current MBA advisor with a proposal: "How about I write my thesis on the topic of 'How to get a PhD in leadership and organizational behavior'?"

My advisor said, "No one has ever done that before, and that's not really research."

"I'll show you how it can be valuable. To get into a doc-toral program, I must figure out what it is I want to research. Answering that part of my application will require me to research what research is and then define my research ques-tion so I can research it during my doctoral program. I propose that half of my thesis is a white paper on identifying a solid research question—even figuring out how people identify a research question in the first place. The other half of the thesis will be a manual explaining what steps must be taken to get into a doctoral program. How about I permit you to use my thesis as a manual for any student who comes after me and wants to continue their education beyond the MBA? Consider my thesis a guidebook and manual to get into a doctoral program. This could be a valuable resource that other schools won't offer to the next generations of students. I'll write my thesis in a way that is instructive for others so that they can use it as a guidebook to advance their life goals."

"We agree to your proposal," the advisor said.

It's always this way with me—figuring out a way to add value to people's lives while also benefiting personally.

The first thing I had to figure out was what professors do. Who better to ask than the professors who authored the articles and textbook chapters that were a part of the MBA curriculum? Two prominent names were listed numerous times across syllabi, and these authors not only researched topics aligned with my leadership interests but also happened to be professors at schools in Boston.

Dr. John Kotter conceived an eight-step change, explained in *Leading Change*.[61] Responding to an email invitation explaining my interests and predicaments—I had no idea how to enter a doctoral program, only that I wanted in!—Dr. Kotter invited me to lunch on the Harvard University campus. (Note: Harvard rejected my application.)

A summary of mostly accurate recollections of my conversations with Dr. Kotter follows. "First, make sure you want to be a PhD. A doctoral program is designed to make you into a researcher and publisher. Your ambition must be to secure lifelong employment by achieving tenure at an AACSB-accredited college of business, and the only way to achieve that goal is to create a body of research that demonstrates your contribution to your chosen field of interest and makes you a highly regarded scholar and subject matter expert. If your ambition is to teach, your MBA will suffice for you to be an adjunct professor as a hobby."

"Jeez. I thought people got a PhD so they could teach. This is new information. I'm interested in answering the question, 'How do we make leaders of all people?' That question has vexed me since my time at INSEAD. It drives me crazy that businesses and organizations, which are run by people, don't invest in the people who run the business and organization. Plus, I think all people are capable of leading. It seems like some people are natural-born leaders while others learn how to lead throughout their lives. Even the people who are perceived by others to be natural-born leaders because they simply take charge or have charming personalities often suck at leading as a result of 'winging it' and never having invested themselves into any leadership development and training. Maybe I can figure out why that is."

To the best of my recollections, Dr. Kotter's responses pointed to the following guidance: "You have a research question in mind. Now, you've got to be willing to spend the rest of your natural life working to figure out the answer to that question, with an unremitting focus on building a body of knowledge around that one tiny little topic that you—and only you—become the world's foremost expert on. The trick is to take what the entire body of research says and learn from people who are looking at this topic from multiple angles to build on their work and find a way to eke out a minor contribution that advances knowledge.

"Once you find your contribution, you must publish articles in the world's top scientific journals. Each paper usually takes three to five years from starting concept, data collection, data analysis, and writing to publication in a blind peer-reviewed academic research journal. The process of writing papers is brutal. Reviewers will read only the words you've put in front of them. In the best-case scenario, you'll have uncovered some nugget of knowledge and communicated it well enough to get back a 'revise and resubmit' of your article, which will cause you to rewrite a great deal of what you wrote and believed to already be amazing and inspiring. Reviewers don't know who you are, and you don't know who they are, and their words cut deep into your heart and mind. You'll experience the highest highs and the lowest lows when you get feedback on your work. Grow a thick skin; that's the only way to make it through the publishing process."

"All that sounds horrible. Why would anyone sign up for that?"

"Great question. Discovering something that helps people and organizations is a noble purpose worth pursuing. I get to say, 'I discovered that!' It's a pretty incredible feeling to do a thing no one in history has done before. The idea that you're responsible for advancing human knowledge is captivating and enticing. I love it," he said.

"Yes! That's what I'm talking about. That's the part that invigorates me. I love it."

"You'll succeed, Bryan. I believe you will one day become a PhD," said Dr. Kotter.

Dr. Kathy Kram was a professor at Boston University (BU). She literally "wrote the book" on the topic of mentoring. Every person who researches mentoring uses her book, *Mentoring at Work: Developmental Relationships in Organizational Life* as gospel.[62] Dr. Kram invited me to her office on BU's campus, and we had a great discussion about what a dissertation on the topic of mentoring might look like. She took a different tack—sage advice from a professor who was trying to make sure I did life right.

My recollection of what Dr. Kram offered to me as development: "Have a real conversation with your partner about the sacrifices you'll have to make. You'll earn almost no money as a PhD student and research assistant. Your lifestyle will change dramatically. Choices must be made about how and with whom you spend your time. The worst thing to happen would be to enter your doctoral program under the misconception that life will be easy. It won't be. You'll be challenged in ways you can't imagine. During those moments when you doubt your decisions, the partner you have at your side will either carry you through or tell you it's okay to quit. Good partners lift you and encourage you to see it through. Speaking of partners in your success, the key to your success will be to find a professor to partner with you in your quest to complete the doctoral program. You'll need an advisor who'll invest their time into your future. For the whole time you're a student, your advisor will become the most important person in your life besides your wife." (Note: BU also rejected my application.)

Kristen and I had long discussions about the sacrifices we'd have to make to persevere through the doctoral program. Kristen said, "I know all these things, Bryan. I knew when I agreed to be your partner in the process and to support you no matter what happens. The most important things are these: Number one, we put our relationship above all else. Number two, you finish, no matter what." We made our commitment to one another to see it through no matter the challenges: financial, emotional, psychological, relational, or the unforeseen.

The next step that I had to take in the application process was to find a needle in a haystack—the aforementioned "advisor." Applicants need someone to be their champion, a unique individual who will guide them at each step of the doctoral program. The worst mistake an applicant can make is submitting their application and saying that they would like to work with a professor with whom they've never actually been in contact with. The key here is to find someone that you have a common interest with, where both your interests align, and you can provide mutual benefit to one another. Having figured out what it was that I wanted to research, the next step was to search the entire planet for the singular professor who did research in the tiny area of leadership that got my motor running. I had to leverage my unabashed willingness to generate connections with strangers and put myself in conversations with professors who were the gatekeepers to my future. Through charm, intellect, courage, character, and wit I would win them over to consider working with me as a doctoral student. I mailed letters, sent emails, and made phone calls to targeted professors that met my criteria. Many of my advances were entirely avoided, others discarded, and others rebuffed with, "thanks but no thanks." I had rejection after rejection. Determined, I kept dialing, just as I had done many years ago in a job as a telemarketer. Funny how skills you pick up along the way in life have a way of resurfacing when you need them the most. My fingers were bleeding when a sliver of hope appeared.

The phone rang. "Hello, this is Dr. Ethlyn Williams," said a female voice with a thick Jamaican accent.

"Greetings, Dr. Williams, my name is Bryan Deptula. I want to study leadership under your mentorship at FAU's PhD program. My research questions are:

- Are leaders born or made?

- How do we make leaders of all people?

"You study presidential elections and leadership during crisis. I'd like to help you with any research projects you have at present. Basically, I'll do whatever you ask to earn a spot in this upcoming cohort of doctoral students."

Dr. Williams said, "Your timing could not be better with the upcoming 2008 presidential election. Each election cycle we research leadership using the presidential election as a time for data collection. Are you willing to collect three hundred responses in a paper survey?"

"Yes, absolutely. Whatever you need, I will do. Send me the survey via email. I will print them out and get them back to you. How much time do I have?"

"Three months. Good luck," said Dr. Williams.

The next day I printed off over five hundred surveys at my own expense. To collect data, I had to ask my MBA professors at Suffolk University if they would allow me to access their classes, distribute the surveys to undergraduate and master's students during class time, and collect the surveys in person. In my mind, and my future depended on it, there was no other way to ensure that I hit the three hundred completed surveys goal. With an average class size of fifteen to twenty people, I approached at least thirty different professors by making unannounced surprise visits during office hours, emailing them, calling, and poking my head into faculty break rooms. It took a month to coordinate a schedule of classes that would give me access to the number of students required. Inconvenient is not a strong enough word to describe the quagmire of class schedules—morning, noon, and night classes for weeks on end. All in I spent over three hundred hours collecting over three hundred surveys.

The only way that I was going to get into a PhD program was to demonstrate my value. Once I had those three hundred surveys in hand, I suddenly became paranoid about shipping them in a box. God forbid they would get lost or destroyed, and with that destruction would come the destruction of my chance at acceptance. I knew those surveys were my golden tickets. So, I protected that box of surveys with my life, purchased a plane ticket to Florida, and hand delivered those golden tickets.

Without knowing the chair (i.e., the boss) of the management department happened to be in Dr. Williams' office, I walked in with my golden tickets, looked these powerful women in the eyes, and said, "I'm Bryan Deptula. I want to get into the PhD program. I need you to know I'm the person who's going to deliver, and here I am delivering to you these three hundred research surveys for the research project I want to be on. I'll succeed. I won't fail. I'm an investment worth making. I flew these surveys down here just to prove how reliable, hardworking, and determined I am to achieve my goals." With that, I triumphantly let the box thud on the desk and allowed silence to fill the air. This moment was very dramatic.

Dr. Williams and I spent the next four hours reviewing the surveys and discussing a plan to turn raw data into new knowledge.

Three weeks later my phone rang with a Boca Raton area code.

"Hello."

"Congratulations. You have been accepted into the upcoming cohort of Florida Atlantic University's PhD program in leadership." *Woo hoo!* "You had better get moving and find a place to live. The program starts in a few months," she said.

Dr. Williams and I have since spent over a decade collaborating on research and coauthored many peer-reviewed journal articles and conference papers, and a book chapter. We have practically never stopped fascinating one another with ideas on what to research next.

Before Kristen and I left Boston, I had one more commitment to honor. A while back, Jacques and the producers of *The Real World* Cancún television show had tried to convince me to be the "boss" on the show; a request I had denied. My loyalty to the company, and to Jacques specifically, however, did lead me to offer myself in a role that would limit my exposure as a cast member and also train the cast members who would work as spring break staff in Cancún for the 2009 season. Jacques had given me an opportunity to start my career in leadership and now was my turn to repay her with a minor personal sacrifice that would create a huge win for her and my former company. If you watch the first episode of the twenty-second season of *The Real World*, you will see me in the front of a conference room at the ME resort in Cancún, training over fifty American and Mexican staff.

With that commitment honored, Kristen and I packed our entire lives and drove to Boca Raton.

A few weeks later, I found myself at the Academy of Management annual conference—where over ten thousand of the world's smartest scholars and businesspeople gather to share research, teach, and learn with and from one another. I was to present a research paper by Dr. Williams, Dr. Raj Pillai—another mentor—Dr. Kevin Lowe, and myself on authentic leadership and charisma during a crisis. There I stood presenting a research paper for the first time, literally before I had taken a single class in my PhD program, and stuttered my way through the whole presentation as beads of sweat ran down my forehead and down the small of my back.

At the presenter's table next to me sat an unassuming fella who chatted me up inquisitively about the paper I was about to present. Little did I know that fella was Dr. Bruce Avolio, a world-famous leadership scholar who has written more books and research articles and contributed more to our leadership knowledge than almost any other person in the last thirty years. A few hours after the presentation, Dr. Avolio found me loitering in a room crowded with people I aspired to be like—professors! He offered well wishes and invited me to a conversation to help me in my journey. True to his word, Bruce has made himself available as a guiding light whenever I ask for his time, meeting with me via phone or video and in person at the University of Washington.

Here's the point: Meeting those professors had been a gift I was totally unaware I'd received. None of them mentioned their almost celebrity status or had anything to gain from meeting with or mentoring me. All were overly generous with their time and did it out of a willingness to give back. Their homes and offices weren't draped in badges of honor or memorabilia from achievements; no awards hung proudly. These humble servants of students dutifully placed themselves in the same stratosphere as everyone else. Absent of ego, they unselfishly gave their time to a fledgling student who dreamed of becoming something better. Given their status, they could have very easily blown me off. I was not their student. Lesser people with greater egos would have kicked me to the curb. Their willingness to meet new people, to learn from a novice, to give me credit when I helped them learn, and to admit they'd made some mistake and were still learning each day—that humility humanized them, making them approachable and likable.

The first two years of coursework in a PhD program are the densest period of study known to any person who dares enter. Core classes in the first bits of a program leave a murderous trail of ungraduated students, tortured souls unable to navigate the turbulent waters of newly formed synapses in a tsunami of terms and definitions, novel jargon, and soul-crushing identity rebuilding. Those determined few who make it past coursework are met with the academic equivalent of the medieval Judas Chair—sitting for the comprehensive exams. Comprehensive exams (comps) test students' knowledge of every core course taken—even if that course was taken several years prior to the exams. Comps test fortitude as much as intellect, culling students whose naive ambition is unsupported by determination and/or intellect.

"You'll never be as smart as you are when you take your comprehensive exams," said Dr. Williams. No truer words were ever spoken. To put this in perspective, a typical syllabus for a single core class listed ten to fifteen journal articles, each comprised of twenty-five to fifty pages, giving an average of three hundred pages weekly of the most complex idiomatic, pedantic, verbose, academically ostentatious, exhibitionist, overtly complex, and scientific language imaginable. Every time I counted the reading list in a new syllabus, my head would tilt back as I imagined myself having to climb the steep ascent up Marble Mountain. Slogging through each article easily chewed up three to five hours of life, effectively a full-time job at forty hours reading for *each* core course.

To put this in perspective, sitting for comprehensive exams requires students to remember the main and the obnoxiously esoteric arguments and findings from every assigned article. It took me six months to reread over sixty thousand pages and relearn material from every core course taken over the two prior years—a Thuy Son mountain of paper studiously climbed. Comps require not regurgitation of information, but rather the minutia of knowing the last names and initials of authors who said a very specific morsel of new knowledge, in which article that morsel was said—on what page of the article—during what year the article was published plus core elements of specific theories, pros and contrary perspectives to each theory, and a rock-solid proposal for future research in all subjects. The finiteness of crafting responses to esoteric interrogatories is akin to recalling the precise radius of a gnat's ass (just to show off, a gnat's ass is 0.0001 inches or one ten-thousandth of one inch) and then having to pontificate on the pros and cons of that ass, why it exists where it does, who disagrees with your arguments, and then propose a novel way to research it anew.

All in, comps vampired ten months of my life—not a single moment of which was spent on Kristen and my yet-to-be-born entrepreneurial idea.

The next mountain range to climb was the dissertation. Or, more appropriately labeled: irritation, mental masturbation, self-flagellation, and frustration. A dissertation is a research-based project that demonstrates your ability to independently conduct research on one or more hypotheses. Dissertations are a combination of procedural submissions, endless revisions, subtractions and additions, data collection, theoretical and empirical writing, ass kissing, political plotting, and mental gymnastics. Students charge headfirst with indefatigable determination into winds of academic hazing by a committee of faculty members in charge of determining the rest of their life. Not a simple goal: discover something that no one has ever researched, suffer through an excruciating review and methodological approval, convince a committee of professors your idea merits two years of their time and attention, such that by approving your dissertation you become a member of the elite group of humans who occupy the ivory tower.

The dissertation is designed to guillotine students who are unwilling to commit themselves to an arduous journey of unanticipated setbacks, and relentless insults from blind reviewers who violate the author's self-confidence. Procedurally, completing a dissertation is exactly the same as creating a research paper for academic journals, and the committee—by extension the university—is endowed with the rights and responsibilities to graduate only those students who demonstrate the temerity and strength of character to continually submit themselves to the tortuous path of writing journal articles—repeatedly—throughout their academic career.

Dissertations, then, are like a trailer preview to the movie that will become your life as an academic. To summit the dissertation, one must push through self-doubt, reach inside themselves to call from within a grin-and-bear-it fortitude, humble themselves to others who control their destiny—all the while not crumbling under pressure. History is replete with quitters who made it through comps but wear the noose of being "all but dissertation" (ABD). Having made it past the comprehensive exams these woeful ABDs could not navigate the land mines that litter the mountainside of the dissertation process. This is why I remind people who flatter me with praise of my title, "Earning a doctorate does not make you any smarter a person than anyone else. It simply means that you are a glutton for punishment who had the perseverance and positive psychological capital (hope, self-efficacy, optimism, resilience)[63] to persist through the death of your previous self, and the soul-crushing identity and brand rebuilding, to birth your future best self."

As if this painful exercise weren't sufficient punishment, I apportioned to myself the work of pushing a camel through the eye of a needle (Matthew 19:24): finding a dissertation topic that would both get approved and could serve as a launching point for the still yet-to-be-born leadership development company that Kristen and I dreamed up. To that end, all the research would have to pass the theoretical and methodological sniff test of the committee. For my business, I would have to translate esoteric theoretical discourse to real and tangible workshops that we could sell as a leadership development program.

Here's a thing that I have discovered repeatedly in life: It is you who must be your best advocate and you also need mentors—people who will advocate for you, who will introduce you to power players and decision-makers, who will give you psychological support when you are down (as happens when you are summiting the mountain of a dissertation and doctoral program), and who will put their name next to yours in promoting your cause.

You are not entitled to anything so you must have mentors to teach and guide you along the way to earn the things you desire, and which will make your life better. To get ahead you must face stiff competition from people who are just as motivated, maybe more motivated, as you are to be the one "admitted" into programs or jobs or promotions and must have a mentor who will lend their credibility and give others reasons to promote you over others. With each successive move in the chess match of life, with each step up the staircase that leads you to the top of the mountain, you must produce in greater measure more than you consume. There are no ways in which you can simply be the recipient of other people's benevolence without putting back into the system something that is of value.

The only way that I could get a PhD was to provide a value and a contribution to the professors who I was going to work with. There was only the benevolence of people who gave me guidance on how to get a PhD that I could rely on.

By integrating myself into academia, I became part of a core group of individuals whose sole pursuit is the advancement of knowledge. Learning from them and understanding how to research correctly allowed me to contribute my own work while collaborating with other brilliant minds. On my own initiative and proactive seeking of information and building relationships was I able to get into a doctoral program.

I am almost never the brightest bulb in the room. My great value to myself and others is my ability to find creative ways to advocate for myself and to demonstrate the value that I bring to any person I meet and organization in which I seek to participate. Completing the dissertation is the last hoop to jump through to complete a PhD program, and I had spent all my energy, all my political goodwill, all my relational maintenance, toward graduating.

Thankfully, I could put into perspective the uphill battles I faced compared to the monumental achievements of those who've come before me. "If I have seen further, it is by standing on the shoulders of giants," said Sir Isaac Newton. If it weren't for the gift of mentoring freely offered by the giants of academia, I couldn't have gone further in my life. When I've seen further, it's by standing on mountains, overlooking water, in moments of peace where I open myself up to the limitless possibilities present in the universe. For, if monks working inside Huyen Khong Cave on Thuy Son Mountain under candlelight could carve out a Buddha three yards in height and almost as wide, it doesn't seem so big a project to earn a PhD.

## WHY YOU SHOULD CARE TO GET A MENTOR

By engaging in mentoring, both mentors and mentees can experience significant neurological benefits that extend far beyond the transfer of knowledge and skills in the immediate context of their professional relationship. At the core of these effects is the release of oxytocin. This neurochemical promotes social bonding, trust, and empathy, enhancing the connection between mentor and mentee while creating an environment conducive to learning and growth.[64] The neurochemical response creates a positive feedback loop, making both mentor and mentee more receptive to learning and collaboration. Studies using hyper scanning have shown that during positive mentoring interactions, the brains of mentors and mentees can exhibit neural synchrony, which is associated with improved communication, enhanced rapport, and more effective knowledge transfer.[65]

Mentoring also engages the brain's social cognition network, including regions like the medial prefrontal cortex and temporoparietal junction, leading to improved ability to understand others' perspectives and better navigation of complex social dynamics in professional settings.[66]

Mentoring creates positive physiological effects. Positive mentoring experiences lead to the achievement of personal and professional goals, which activates the brain's reward system and the neurotransmitter dopamine that increases motivation, enhances memory formation, and improves focus. Additionally, effective mentoring relationships can help regulate cortisol, resulting in reduced stress and anxiety levels and improved cognitive performance under pressure.[67]

Long-term involvement in mentoring relationships can strengthen the connectivity among different brain regions, leading to more integrated cognitive processing and enhanced creative problem-solving skills.[68] Additionally, the reflective practices common in mentoring (like those found in self-leadership)—such as examining past experiences or future goals—engage the brain's default mode network, improving self-reflection, introspection, and the ability to learn from past experiences.[69] The same mirror neuron system that is critical in self-leadership also plays a role in mentoring relationships. During highly productive mentoring interactions, mirror neurons allow mentees to internalize behaviors, skills, and attitudes modeled by their mentors, facilitating rapid skill transfer and enhancing empathy.[70]

Engaging in mentoring activities strengthens the prefrontal cortex, the brain region responsible for executive functions; this leads to improved decision-making abilities, enhanced emotional regulation, and better strategic thinking.[71]

Mentoring is good for your career and creates an easy way for you to gain access to esteemed colleagues who will help you develop your leadership skills. Mentoring is also good for your brain. Whether you are the mentor or the mentee, you are not just building your professional network—you are literally rewiring your brain for success and wellbeing.

Having a mentor is not just a nice-to-have thing; it is a career-changing must-have. Research consistently shows that individuals with mentors get more promotions, higher compensation, and greater benefits and get more frequent raises than their mentorless peers.[72] Your mentor becomes your personal career guide, opening doors you didn't even know existed and introducing you to the people with the power in organizations who can turbocharge your professional trajectory. They are not just teaching you how to do your job; they are schooling you how to navigate office politics and showing you how to get ahead in the organizational chart. Your mentor protects you from people who covertly sabotage you and endorses you to power players who decide your future, providing a shield against workplace drama and lending you credibility. But it is not all about climbing the organizational ladder. Mentors provide psychosocial support that boosts your confidence, helps you develop a stronger professional identity, and enhances your overall job satisfaction.

Having a mentor is absolutely crucial in our postpandemic, work-from-wherever world. The pandemic has disrupted our ability to think collaboratively and leverage collective intelligence in traditional workplace settings, lessening creative problem-solving and innovation; mentoring relationships can provide a vital cognitive outlet, stimulating intellectual discourse that counteracts this isolation-induced cognitive stagnation.

In the face of the COVID-19 pandemic shift from in-office to remote workers, mentors may play a critical role in helping individuals navigate the unique challenges of virtual collaboration and digital fatigue, offering strategies honed through their own experiences. Social isolation resulting from remote work has led to feelings of disconnection and loneliness among many professionals, affecting their sense of belonging and team cohesion; mentors can serve as a crucial social anchor, providing not just professional guidance but also much-needed human connection and emotional support, helping to alleviate these feelings of isolation. In an era where face-to-face interactions are limited, mentors become essential in maintaining a sense of connection to the workplace and fostering a feeling of belonging.

Career progression has become more challenging in the postpandemic era, with reduced visibility in remote settings potentially leading to missed opportunities; mentors can play a pivotal role in keeping mentees connected to organizational networks, advocating for their visibility, and guiding them through the nuanced landscape of career advancement in a transformed work environment. They offer guidance on maintaining visibility and relevance within the organization, ensuring that remote workers are not overlooked for opportunities due to their physical absence.[73] A mentor serves as a vital link to the organizational culture and informal networks that are often lost in virtual environments.[74] They provide invaluable insights into the nuanced changes in company dynamics and priorities that may be difficult to discern from a distance.

Moreover, mentors provide much-needed emotional support and perspective during times of uncertainty. They can help mentees develop resilience and adaptability, crucial skills in a rapidly changing work environment. As organizations continue to evolve in response to pandemic-induced changes, mentors can assist in interpreting new policies, adapting to shifting expectations, and identifying emerging opportunities within the transformed landscape of work.[75]

As a leader, it is your responsibility to both be a mentor and encourage your employees to find their own mentor. For all the reasons listed above, you and your followers are better when all support one another with mentoring. The path to exceptional leadership is paved with continuous learning and growth. By embracing mentoring relationships, you are not just investing in your own development, but also contributing to the growth of others. Whether you are seeking a mentor or stepping into the role of one, remember that these relationships have the power to transform careers, organizations, and lives. In the end, the knowledge you gain, the connections you make, and the impact you have on others will far outweigh any investment of time or effort.

## A PERSONAL NOTE

I share my journey of pursuing advanced degrees not because I believe everyone should follow the same path, but to emphasize the importance of continuous learning. My decision to invest years in research and become an authority in my field was driven by a deep commitment to being a valuable resource for others. While you may not want or need to make such extreme sacrifices, you should be passionate about becoming your best self as a leader. This requires a dedication to learning, whether through formal education, mentoring relationships, self-study, or on-the-job experiences. The truth is, I do not wish my experiences getting a PhD on anyone. During my PhD process, my brain was literally rewired, and I could feel the torture of rebuilding my identity. It was hard and it really sucked for a great percentage of time. That said, it was my path, and I earned that degree because of my own drive and the care of a great many mentors who believed in me.

Now that I am a doctor, the only prescription I give to you is to take a healthy dose of nutrition (learning from anywhere) and exercises (apply what you learn at your job and in your home) to build your mentoring muscles.

# E = ENTREPRENEUR

## (HOW TO THINK AND ACT
## LIKE AN ENTREPRENEUR)

# 10

## ENTREPRENEUR:
## A LOGICAL CONCLUSION

Ski Hill Road in Leavenworth, Washington, is a slightly sloping road with the most pristine scenic mountains views a person could dream to rest their eyes upon. Formerly the site of the U.S. ski jumping championships in 1941, 1959, 1967, 1974, and 1978, Leavenworth averages ninety-five inches of snowfall accumulation annually. Visitors to Ski Hill now enjoy a family-oriented gently sloping beginner's hill, tubing on a rope pulled line, and a nostalgic wooden cabin that houses a supersized open fireplace: a fireplace reminiscent of Christmas movies where everyone comes in from the snow and rubs their hands together to warm up as they drink hot cocoa. With gorgeous lodge-style homes lining the roads leading up to the mountain adventure area, Ski Hill forms part of a several-mile-loop that allows people to saunter at their own pace, soaking in the sunbeams reflected off gleaming pillows of snow that rise to heights that dwarf the tallest person. So serene it is, that people often find themselves pondering their place in life, what it all means, and how they fit into the creator's grand plan.

Growing up in Leavenworth, Kristen learned to ski on Ski Hill Mountain. Before she could tie her own shoes, little Kristen tucked poles under her arms as she rocketed down neighboring ski resorts such as Stevens Pass on death-defying double black diamond runs with names like Big Chief. Along with becoming an avid skier, she had accustomed herself to long hikes up and across the miles of terrain surrounding Leavenworth and Ski Hill Mountain. Kristen's eyes would look toward the heavens, her head tilted as she recollected fondly of moments where life's questions had been discerned amid the sounds of tree branches relieving themselves of the burden of white pressure, and snow being crushed under waffle-shaped contraptions atop her winter boots.

"Answers await you in the moments when you are most open to receiving nature," Kristen said to me as I was studying during visits to her Grandma Marydell's home. "Listen to the quiet. The mountains are talking to you." During my doctoral program, on reunion vacations, Grandma Marydell's ceiling-to-floor window served as a portal to a natural mountainous landscape; it was a see-through barrier between the heated comfort of modern living and the brutality of winter at three thousand feet above sea level. There were uninterrupted views of slightly iced-over rivers whose genesis flowed from peaks that pierced the veil of cloud cover. There was an absence of anything made by humans. Raptors—the powerful kings of birds of prey—such as bald eagles scan the skyline, red-tailed hawks glide over vast territories searching for unsuspecting creatures, and ospreys circle bodies of water awaiting the perfect moment for a dive and catch. Moments of peace transcend time.

Finding myself dry-eyed from a deep unconscious stare, my thoughts shifted effortlessly among the myriad subjects bursting from pages of articles and books and the infinite possibilities that inspire the human soul to explore the great outdoors. The vast expanse of open space continues onward, outward, everywhere. Open space ad infinitum, a limitless geography and symbol of limitless opportunity. Sky is not the limit, only part of rising space awaiting with welcome arms. *Incoming call.* "Go on, young man. Remove human-made walls—both real and imagined. Dream. Be big. Be bold. Dare to climb. Your purpose, not found, yet findable," said the mountain.

Cues from God, divined though the mountains as an instrument of a whispering voice so many times in the history of humankind, are sometimes thinly shrouded to require deep contemplation to discern their meaning; other times, as now, cues are so loud they shout at you with enough force to burst your eardrums. Moses received the Ten Commandments on Mount Sinai, or more traditionally known as Jabal Musa (Exodus 19:2; 24:16). Jesus Christ spoke his lengthiest sermon atop the Mount of Beatitudes (Matthew 5-7), was transfigured on what is now named the Mountain of Transfiguration (Matthew 17:1–8, Mark 9:2–8, Luke 9:28–36), died on the cross at Calvary (Matthew 27:33, Mark 15:22, Luke 23:33, John 19:17), and then ascended to heaven from the Mount of Olives as his disciples gathered in miraculous observation (Acts 1:9–12).

The prophet Muhammad several times climbed Mount Hira, whereupon the first verses of the Koran were revealed to him. Shiva and Parvati, Hindu deities, are thought to domicile for eternity in Mount Kailash; the same mountain Bon, Buddhism, and Jainism believe is sacred.

Mountains give promise to those who endeavor to climb them, to see the world from a different view, to literally get out on the vista. Serving as powerful echo chambers for the sender of messages, mountains give home to those seeking answers to change the human experience—the receivers of messages. Having heard or divined a communication to share, mountains are the place to make pronouncements, to shout it from the mountaintops.

"Let's go for a walk around Ski Hill," Kristen said, at the very moment my own listening to the mountain had passed.

"Wow. I was just about to say that."

"A walk will be good for us. You need a break from studying anyhow. You haven't looked at your schoolwork for over an hour. Grandma and I watched you. Your lips were moving, quietly, in whisper. Who were you talking to, looking out to the mountains?" she asked.

"The mountains and I were talking, I suppose. Got me thinking about where we are headed next in life. Looking at these mountains, everything seems possible. You ever get that feeling?"

Kristen said, "Of course, I spent my whole life in these mountains. The mountains inspired me to travel. They led me to you."

Wanderlust struck about half a mile into our hike. "It's incredible up here. I love it, being in the mountains opens my spirit. Makes me think we can do so much more with our lives than we are doing."

"You are not fulfilled," Kristen said. She was looking at me with one eyebrow pointed toward the mountain peak and the other bent in a pinched squint that formed crow's-feet on her temple.

"Whadda ya mean I am not fulfilled? I am happy and fulfilled. Marriage is super fun. My doctoral program—also going great. We recently passed multiple major life milestones; the result of a plan set in motion years prior. We're established in our new life, a mix of financial sacrifice, new geography, and more certain than before speeding through the milestones and a little less uncertain than a sailboat in a windstorm without a rudder. We were moving forward, fast, but in what direction? Where to next?"

Kristen said, "No, you're not. You're antsy. Smoke is coming from your ears. The wheels are already in motion, so you had best just say what it is that you are strategizing."

To this day, Kristen knows my inner workings light-years ahead of when I come to the conclusions she's already concluded. As partners in a relationship, we are good at envisioning our future and making it happen; it is the result of hours upon hours of intimate conversations trying to figure out where we want to go in life, what we need to sacrifice, how to get there stepwise, and her knowing my restless spirit was no sooner fulfilling one life's dream than it was looking over a body of water divining what will be the next mountain to climb.

"You are right. The whole point of getting the PhD was so that we can live the life that we want to live, not beholden to any job or person. We have sacrificed so much to gain independence. Academia is rigid, hierarchical, and linear. In two years' time, I start the search for a professor job. The year after that, we'll move to a university city, most likely not of our choosing or preference, just to get a job as a professor. Kids will come thereafter.

"What I have learned thus far into my program, however, is that being a professor does not give you any autonomy other than to pick the eighty hours a week that you want to work. I will spend many hours by myself researching and writing academic articles that no one will read. Here's a statistic that I can't get my head around, in terms of whether anything I do as a scholar makes a difference. Guess the modal number that a published academic article is cited by anyone other than the original author. Zero—not kidding. Professors are not rewarded and are nearly disincentivized to be great teachers. Thus, less time in a classroom changing lives and more time alone writing is the only way to climb the ivory tower.

"It all seems kind of pointless. That is, unless I can make practical use of my research. Use the research to drive the teaching, but not in a classroom. I want to do it for people outside the university system, maybe get back to my roots as a corporate trainer and keynote speaker."

"You still want to be in front of people, speaking your truth, which is that you care about people, want them to be better. So, you want to start a leadership training and development company?"

Insightful. Surmising. Pointed. Clear. Kristen says in two sentences what it took me four months and a half mile up a mountain to articulate.

"Yes. We need a company of our own. Raising kids is not a part-time job that we should do after work and on weekends. I want us to really raise our kids, our way, full of travel, life experiences adding to our guiding and the formal school education. Plus, when I have a PhD and you don't, then we're not actually independent, are we? You will have to get a job working for someone else, and we're back where we started—two-week vacations, crappy bosses, office politics. The American corporate life is not for us. But, we are indeed headed toward the life that has come to pass as tolerable in American culture. We don't want that life. By God and all these birds that are circling us, we will not be the tormented, stressed out, "hating-my-life-in-an-office" worker bees that society pushes us to be. We will make the lives of others better while making our own lives better."

"Let's do it. Makes perfect sense. I can run the marketing and operations. You focus your research on leadership and mentoring. Everything you read and publish can be translated from theory into practice. Our product will be workshops and keynotes that you create based on your own best practices and research, and that of other scholars, consultants, and practitioners. You are your best self, and are energized, when you give people the tools and knowledge to become their own best selves."

> *Entrepreneurial mindset is demonstrated in one's belief that they would be an entrepreneur, and all outcomes associated with owning his/ her own business would be due to their own influence on the cause and effect of their own decision-making and effort.*

Kristen has an entrepreneurial mindset built into her from a lineage of entrepreneurs. We passed a parcel of land under her own family ownership. Grandma and Grandpa spent sixty years in marriage and entrepreneurship, building a lumber business in the state of Washington. Grandpa had, as family lore tells, rode a horse over the Cascade Mountains, from Leavenworth to Seattle, and dragged back lumber to build the young couple's first house.

Leftover wood from the construction sat outside their property with no good use. A stranger passed by and said, "What are you going to do with that wood? If you're not going to use it, I will buy it from you." Days later, Grandpa built a shed and hung a shingle that read: "Wood for sale." Grandma counted the dollar bills, and they were off to business.

Kristen was entrepreneurial by spirit and blood, fearing nothing of the risks that she had many times witnessed her kin work through with industry. Starting our own company, in her mind, was as foregone a conclusion as was finishing the PhD in my own mind.

"When do we start?"

"You start creating content now. I will start working on branding and marketing. When you finish the degree, first things first, we'll launch."

"Where?"

"Maybe, instead of you becoming a professor, we move to Key West? We're only a few hours' drive. The move would be easy and there is lots of tourism to support the business. We'll host corporate retreats together with wellness and yoga retreats. You will be the speaker and trainer. Tourism will keep the business running until we get the leadership training and development division up and running. We're in the Keys a couple times a month. Stone crab festivals. Fantasy Fest. Sunset and sailboats. Cuban coffee in shacks on the side of the road, run by little ladies who shuffle among locals and tourists. Key West has great infrastructure. There are plenty of bed and breakfasts or inns that we can convert into a resort and retreat paradise. Other than Rehoboth Beach, there is no better place on the East Coast to put all the pieces together."

Just like that, the whole vision and mission. The next fifteen years of our lives would be based on a discussion had while on a two-mile hike up a mountain on Ski Hill Road.

Over the next few days, we noodled on the idea and set a plan in place such that everything I researched and read about during my PhD program would contribute to building a leadership and personal development business. Our mission: enrich the lives of others by helping them pull from within themselves the leader that they already were but didn't know that they were—to help people see the leader within.

I would focus my research on specific areas of leader development, identity formation, people's motivation to lead, and how to give them practical tools that they could use at home and at the office. The academic peer-reviewed papers that I coauthored would feed the content of the keynotes and workshops. The fundamental strategic point of differentiation that we sought to create and capitalize on, was that I would publish academically peer-reviewed journal articles based on content that I really loved, content focused on the practical application of theoretically driven leadership research. I was fascinated by how one person—a professor, speaker, trainer, mentor, leader—could improve employees' lives in the workplace by helping them be better at what they do at work. Those skills, if the trainee were paying attention, easily translate into personal skills to improve quality of life.

Kristen said, "What's our value proposition? What differentiates us from every other company or person claiming to develop leaders? Everyone who's ever had a manager's role believes themselves to be a subject matter expert on leadership. They're wrong. You can't be a leadership expert just because you held a manager's job or got a coaching certificate. How do we cut through all the pretenders to show we/you are the real deal? There are lots of snake oil salespeople, and we need to show that working with us creates a better ROI than working with other companies.

"We must answer the question, 'Why work with Bryan and our team?' Everyone knows leaders suck. Now, we show them you're the solution to help executives and managers lead better. You're a doctor—and your patients are organizational leaders.

"What makes you different from all other consultants, speakers, and training companies is that you are an expert. You're an authority who has done primary research and written peer-reviewed articles on leadership, management, and organizational behavior—someone who owns his own company and has been in the trenches of private and public companies. You're one of the few people who is a theoretical scholar and a practitioner who knows how to run a business—and train people to lead organizations to growth and profitability. Bryan, you're a unicorn."

Agreed. Here's why our company is different: First and most importantly, I'm a PhD and subject matter expert who's spent his entire life researching, writing, teaching, and speaking about leaders, leading, leadership, and the power of self-belief as the foundation of improving the quality of one's life. My goal is to make the world a better place by using my God-given gifts and tools to affect the lives and leadership of all people positively.

Second, we need to clarify the misinformation people receive. The problem is that only academics read academic research. That means businesspeople and humans everywhere either don't have access to or don't take the time to educate themselves on research. Most people would rather read an article written by someone without leadership knowledge but who somehow anoints themselves a leadership expert because they can write a blog post or book. It's infuriating. Too many leadership trainers and speakers make empty promises, and when companies pay for training, they get zero results.

Third, we need to give executives a reason to believe that by investing in their employees, the executives benefit financially. Research suggests executives sometimes need to drive extra earnings to justify their compensation.[76] We can help executives by giving them a reason to pay for training: a huge ROI.

When I deliver a workshop today, the lessons learned affect tomorrow's work and have a gigantic positive effect on performance six months or a year down the road. In a world where quarterly stock report expectations corner executives, they expect to see immediate ROI.

Fourth, we must deliver the types of programs clients want and need. We'll conduct market research by asking clients:

- What do you want to know?

- What kind of leadership training does your company need?

- What are the most common leadership challenges you face at each organizational level: frontline, middle management, executive?

- What kind of training would you be willing to pay for?

- What competencies, knowledge, skills, and abilities do you want your emerging leaders to learn?

- What decision-making criteria do you use when spending money on training and development?

Because I'd spent over a decade researching the topic, refining our workshops, and creating super fun, high-energy, motivational keynotes and experiential retreats, we'd identified our strategic and first-mover advantages. Our product emerged, giving our company a clear path forward. We quickly created, copyrighted, and sold a series of workshops titled "Leaders Are Born To Be Made."

From the top of the mountain, one can simultaneously see the whole world and want to change it magnanimously. Amid the daydreaming, gazing into the great yonder, and pontificating on how amazing our company would be, it dawned on us that neither Kristen nor I had ever started a company from scratch. Sure, I had been a great individual contributor, a leader in multiple companies, created my own divisions as extensions of existing business units, innovated, and trained. None of that was for a company over which I had sole control, assuming all the risk and some of the reward. Worse, realizing my imposter syndrome, I was in academia researching and publishing on leadership and mentoring, and teaching undergraduate business courses. Turned out, I didn't know the first thing about starting a business. The road to becoming a successful entrepreneur is long, steep, and up a mountain hill with no safety net. *Huh. Who knew?*

Just as Kristen and I dreamed our new business idea into the realm of the possible, I was summiting the dissertation and found myself at base camp of the job search. The search for a full-time professor position, which unto itself is like finding a needle (a position that suits one's specific area of knowledge) in a haystack (universities, most of which are in towns you've never heard of), usually takes eighteen months from interview to job start. The natural sequencing of a doctoral program dictates that students simultaneously work toward completion of the dissertation while looking for a job; ideally graduating as a PhD in May, and subsequently starting their new job as a faculty member the following August. Fortunately, I was hired at Central Washington University in Seattle, where we relocated in 2013 at the conclusion of my fourth year, officially in purgatory of the aforementioned "all but dissertation" status.

"What does it show? Tell me! Are there two lines?"

"*Yes!* We're pregnant," Kristen said.

"Woo hoo! I love you so much. We're gonna have a baby. Holy mother of God. We're having a child."

Our baby grew in Kristen's womb within a few weeks of our arrival to Seattle, before we found permanent residence. Kristen recently had begun a high-powered position at Starbucks head-quarters in the global communications department, a few offices away from its famous CEO. She was learning about the entrepreneurial spirit that elevated Starbucks to its current status and building on years of her own experience in public relations. With a baby on the way, we needed long-term financial stability while we nurtured our neonatal business.

Academia, like all exclusive clubs, puts in place a series of hurdles, barricades, and hoops for the aspirants seeking membership to jump over and through. Just when you believe you have made it into this exclusive club, the powers that be put in front of you a series of hurdles significantly more difficult than getting through your doctor program. Unlike almost every other profession, academia has institutionalized a famously torturous double-edged sword that offers the promise of lifelong employment called "tenure"—or your job and career get axed. Pressure is immense because the consequences of achieving or failing to earn tenure are enormous. Achieve tenure and you'll enjoy permanent, lifelong, guaranteed employment. Fail to get tenure at one university, and become stigmatized within academia, subjugated to rumor mills and relegated to the ranks of lower-esteemed community colleges and for-profit faux universities.

Cold, calculated, and politically motivated, the tenure and promotion process is a stress-filled yearlong evaluation that takes place at the end of a professor's fifth year of employment. Realistically, a newly hired professor's "tenure clock" starts ticking their first day on the job. Professors put together a package that describes their previous five years of work—and a promise of the next five years—replete with every intellectual contribution, journal article, conference presentation, student evaluation of teaching, service to the university and community, and a self-authored letter that walks a razor-thin line between humility and absolute self-aggrandizement. Teaching and service affect the tenure decision very little. Either you *publish* more than the minimum number of peer-reviewed research articles, in high-ranking journals—thereby establishing yourself as a creator of new knowledge and subject matter expert in your field—or you *perish*, your name never to be uttered in the hallways of higher education.

*I must get tenure.* Before having finished my dissertation I was in my first year as a professor with the tenure clock ticking. Complicating my motivation was my growing resentment toward endless research requirements. Laboring on my dissertation, which was the very thing, my own research agenda and ideas, that should have invigorated me toward its completion, was a hard slog of work that, only after hours of prepping myself for the imminent mental obstacle course and brain drain, would I then grudgingly enter.

Dr. Williams reminded me with love, and a wee threat: "I'm willing to invest as much energy into your development as you are willing to put into your own development. Do not ever let there be a time when my caring for your success is more than your own caring for your own success." Stomach ulcers and anxiety are common in those who apply for tenure, because they have put their whole hopes and dreams into this one basket of possibilities. It was not that way for me. Life experiences always have a way putting things into perspective. *I got this. I haven't had a decent night's sleep in six years, but I'm me, right? After all the horrors I have lived through, I can survive a thorough vetting of my performance. No tenure, no problem. PhD for life. I have already quit two different careers to begin this third career. I constantly reinvent myself, and now, I have the title, knowledge, skills, abilities, and experiences to lay my own yellow brick road by building our company.*

As if this torment we're not enough, Kristen and I thought throwing gas on the fire would be a good idea and began work in earnest to launch our entrepreneurial bid. Starting a company is uncomplicated, but it takes several steps, which the unfamiliar can easily overlook. Legal requirements fulfilled, website purchased, and over $10,000 out-of-pocket business start-up expenses paid, BKD Partners, LLC, was officially launched.

Kristen created all the branding for the company: logos, fonts, colors, imagery, and look and feel. I created content, workshops, exercises, workbooks, assessments, keynote speeches, and pricing. We both dove into business development, strategy, and finding places where we could try out the workshops with some paying—but mostly nonpaying—speaking engagements. We were, as it seemed, climbing mountains in every direction.

No sane person would do what we were doing: simultaneously climbing three Ski Hill Mountain peaks—in what was technically my fifth year in the doctoral program in Boca Raton, I was working full-time as a professor in Seattle, and we had taken it upon ourselves to launch our company; I had literally three full-time jobs, each requiring a minimum fifty-hour work week. Plus, we needed to begin nesting for the small matter of bringing a new life into the world. We were drinking change through a firehose.

Rites of passage such as university commencements serve as gateways to clubs that people seek to join. Official and ornamental, ceremonies document a person's transformation and transfiguration from something they weren't, into something that they now are. Commencement ceremonies are full of pomp and circumstance. Soon-to-be graduates have climbed the mountains of requirements before summiting the graduation stage where one's name is called by a university official who declares that a person has completed all coursework and is, through the rights and privileges assigned to the board of trustees, now a graduate.

In May 2013, my five-hundred-plus-page dissertation was approved in a virtual meeting that included me at my office in Seattle and four committee members: two in Florida, one in California, and another in New Zealand.

Two weeks after my dissertation was fully accepted, my name was called by the commencement speaker in front of twenty thousand people at FAU Arena, to an empty seat with a placard reserving my official new title: Dr. Bryan Joab Deptula. The announcement was made to none of the uproarious applause received for other graduates. Two thousand miles away I lay comfortably with my ear on Kristen's bulging stomach as she lay on her back, unable to see her toes beyond the sphere of her tummy. *Whoosh. Whoosh. Whoosh.* Glowing inside, I listened to our baby's heartbeat boom within the womb.

Less than three weeks after the university commencement that transformed me into Dr. Deptula, after Kristen's indefatigable sixty hours of labor, we welcomed our first child into the world. I was now a part of the parent club, a rite of passage that made all my prior selfish endeavors pale in comparison to the joy of transforming into a father.

Sleep deprivation. Crying. Hazy days and nights. Poop. Wipes. Swaddling. Feedings. Twenty-four hours of nonstop energy dedicated to baby. All of my attention, love, and effort went directly into wife and child. A year into parenthood, we spent more time and money on diapers than we did in our business. Then Kristen was pregnant again. Baby number two was on the way.

"Get ready, Bryan. We've got another two papers to write for the Academy of Management conference," Dr. Williams said. And with comments like those, I would squirrel away my time researching fifty hours a week, plus be a dad, plus teach courses on campus. I was hell-bent on getting tenure, to provide a secure financial future that eluded my younger self. The safety net of permanent employment was a strong gravitational pull toward tenure. The rub, though, was having to write research, a grizzly affair for me. I loved the reading and designing of research, analyzing data, and pontificating on results. That was the fun stuff. The torture, though, was sitting by myself, locked away from my baby and pregnant wife, writing scholarly journal articles in a language that seemed foreign and was disagreeable to my natural way of thinking.

Research itself seemed very necessary for making progress in the field, but the act of producing research for me was like laying on a bed of broken glass and then having someone pour acid over my cuts. As an extrovert, I give and receive energy from engaging with people. As a researcher, I, like every other scholar, is forced to spend absorbent time alone reading and writing. Academic writing is hard. It is a brutal affair calling forth the most difficult process for explaining one's thoughts.

Writing itself is generally enjoyable to me—for example the writing of this book was loads of fun—but academic writing requires a level of sophistication and finesse to make extraordinarily difficult theoretical arguments sound interpretable and readable. The whole thing for me just sucked.

The more I wrote the less I liked what I was doing; and the further I got away from actually doing what I wanted to do, which was to build our company with me at the front as a speaker to people and businesses. With people, working as an educational tour guide, doing the hard work of changing lives, applying leadership lessons of my own creation, extrapolated from the best practice leaders and brightest scholars—that's my happy place.

So, there I was, spending hundreds of hours a month locked away from the people I loved, writing in a foreign language from an alien invader, teaching in a basement classroom the content that I had no hand in creating. I did not like how I was spending my time. I grew irritable, disgruntled. Getting a PhD and becoming a professor and scholar is a natural career path, but it was not the career path for me. Revelations abounded: turns out, I like being a professor, but what I like more is being in charge of my own destiny and earning potential.

"Are we making any money? Because we are spending a lot," Kristen said.

"Generating revenue: yes. Making money: no. We're still spending more than we're making. Building a brand takes a long time."

Kristen said, "I get that. We are at the point where we need to make decisions about the future of this company and our family. You are burnt out, and becoming, yet again, frustrated. We barely see you because you are traveling so much, and when we do see you, you're no fun. You cannot keep up this pace or you'll have a breakdown. We either ramp up this company—and you find investors—or you find happiness being a professor."

Seeking investors was new to me. Having the gift of gab is a useful tool for speakers, only insofar as the gab is filled with useful information. Crafting my investor pitch deck, I realized very quickly that I had not thought through many of the key bits of information needed by investors. I traveled around the country trying to convince potential investors that we were growing a company that would deliver ROI.

"What's your product? Seriously, what are you selling, other than you lecturing in front of a bunch of people like you're in a college classroom? You don't have anything but a bunch of PowerPoint presentations. You have no product. If you were anyone else who came in my office with this crap presentation, I would have thrown them out. Because you are refining your product, no two presentations are alike. Right now, you should work on defining the product. Use every speaking engagement to try out messaging. Figure out what you and only you can say to people. Speak your truth, reveal sacred parts of yourself to clients. Use the audience in product development research. Pour your heart and soul into perfecting your craft," said an investor who declined.

In another meeting, where I was sure that my pitch was as smelly as the bottom side of a toilet, a potential angel investor quickly rebuffed my advances while doling out of this nugget: "You need to bootstrap this company. Bootstrapping is a process where entrepreneurs invest their own money in their start-up, with no outside investors. You sell a few things, reinvest that money immediately into the company, improve the product and marketing; then you sell a little more, invest a little more, in an endless cycle where the hope is that you'll make a little bit more money than you are investing. One day, if you figure out what problem you're solving for the world, people will vote for your product with their dollars. You will eventually pull some money out of the company for yourself. You're smart. You'll figure it out."

The problem with pinpointing the outcome of leader development is that humans take time to develop. I might deliver a workshop today that affects tomorrow's work by a fraction of the gigantic positive impact the workshop will have on performance six months or a year down the road. In a world where executives are cornered by quarterly stock report expectations, their desire is to see immediate ROI. I had to sell myself as the solver of a problem that companies had yet to identify.

As a newly graduated PhD my favorite new hobby was babbling on about some new solution to a problem that I had just learned. Time and again I would find myself talking incessantly only to look at my audience staring straight into an infinite sea with glazed-doughnut eyes. Some folks wouldn't even feign interest, literally letting their head fall back as they looked up at the ceiling in total boredom.

Given that I was trying to impress high-level executives so that they would see the value in my services, this was not the response I wanted. After months of crushing rejection, insecurity stemming from the deafening sound of silence of a nonringing business phone, I invited a mentor to lunch. Upon explaining my frustration at the slow start of our newly launched company, his grin widened like the Cheshire Cat in *Alice's Adventures in Wonderland*. His inner satisfaction grew in direct proportion with my curiosity. He said, "People don't care how much you know until they know how much you care."

My mentor revealed to me a pearl of wisdom that changed my life. I falsely believed that my credentials gave me credibility. So, I pivoted from *telling and selling* to the market, what I thought it needed: *better leaders*. And I pivoted to conducting market research by asking clients: "What do you want to know? What type of leadership training does your company need? What are the most common leadership challenges you face at each organizational level: front line, middle management, executive? What kind of training would you be willing to pay for? What competencies, knowledge, skills, abilities do you want your emerging leaders to learn?"

Then, instead of talking, a pesky trait to which I am preternaturally inclined, I started listening; hearing the essence of the questions, the innuendos, overt curiosities, and most importantly, the decision-making criteria decision-makers used when deciding to spend money on training and development.

We were celebrating our small modicum of a breakthrough while sipping cocktails in South Beach in Miami Beach with a British friend who happened to be visiting us. Kristen said, "Finally, headway. How do we bring legitimacy to this concept? We need to get the word out on the biggest possible stage."

Our British friend quickly said, "Bryan should do a TED Talk."

"Huh? I wouldn't know the first thing about how to apply. However, 'leaders are born to be made' makes a great topic."

"Go for it, mate. People need the answer to this question," he said.

Through divine providence or serendipity, a week later I received in my NSU email: "TEDx Talk—Apply Now." Unbeknownst to me, NSU independently produced an annual TEDx event. On the strength of the leaders are born to be made topic, I applied, was interviewed in person on the nature and content of the talk, and was selected to be one of six presentations that would create the next series of TEDx Talks. My TEDx Talk launched in 2018.

One minute I was like every other schmuck peddling leadership development, but the very moment that my name was associated with TEDx Talk, my credibility skyrocketed. We started receiving requests for me to do speaker series, keynotes, and corporate development workshops. We were now catching instead of pitching.

This lit within me a fire to fulfill my life's purpose: be a guide by the side of people in their pursuit of personal development, wellness, and a better life, and to lead by example and speak with wisdom that immediately and dramatically improves people's quality of work performance and personal life.

I used to say, "I want to make the world a better place." That always seemed overly dramatic to me, too amorphous to quantifiably measure my impact. From the moment I started preparing for my TEDx Talk, I realized that my goal was to make the life of one person better, and then the next person's life better, and the next, until the day I die. Measuring my impact one life at a time is a better lens through which to observe life.

Personal choices nurtured professional opportunity. The birth of our second child further cemented our decision that Kristen would be a stay-at-home mom. Between breast-feeding and naps, Kristen rejuvenated her professional identity over the first three years of our daughter's life by creating our business development and marketing collateral, building our network and database, finding me paid and pro bono speaking gigs at a clip of about forty per annum, and sharing our vision, mission, and values with a world of clients.

I was giving academic presentations at the Academy of Management at a pace of four per year. Research from my dissertation, along with articles on presidential leadership and charismatic leadership that were led by Dr. Williams, were published. With enough research to secure me a promotion to associate professor at NSU, we cranked up the volume of speaking to twice monthly major state or national events. I joined the Vistage speaker circuit, developed a series of four-hour workshops that were to be delivered to executive peer coaching groups, and delivered eighteen workshops to different groups across America. Finally, we had a product, credibility, and consumer demand. Bootstrapped. Booyah!

It was right about this time that I received the phone call. "Bryan, this is NSU's provost."

"Good day, sir. How can I help you?" Famous last words.

The provost said, "You have been nominated by your peers to be the acting department chair for the College of Business, Management Department. This is a great honor to be nominated by your peers, and NSU needs you."

"I'm flattered. Candidly, I have never desired a leadership position in academia, and have not put myself forward for any such candidacy." Department chair is a thankless and difficult job: the equivalent of trying to herd the world's smartest and most powerful cats.

"How about you do it for one year and then we reassess. I asked around. You're the guy and this is the moment," the provost said. My vanity was stroked that my peers had nominated me for such a post. Naturally, I acquiesced and had the privilege of serving as acting chair for a year: a new challenge that gave me access for over a year to the internal workings of the university and leadership experience among an excellent faculty.

Something had to give. Practically, my dance card was full, and our business was growing. We had more speaker requests than we could possibly resource. My life consisted of home-airport-plane-hotel-deliver a workshop-return home-chair the department-meetings-business development-raising two children-maintain commitment to a loving wife and business partner.

"This is ridiculous," Kristen said. She opened the door to another life planning session. "OMG. We are both totally exhausted. We're both giving away bits of ourselves to everyone and everything, and we're missing out on the good quality time with the kids. We have no support system to help us. We don't have enough money at this point to hire anyone for the company. No family lives in Florida. No support for us to raise the kids. Plus, we have got to get the kids into a K-12 school system where they will stay. How long do you see us staying in Florida?"

She said, "Please, pick a path. I need to either get a full-time job or you need to commit to our company. We have worked so hard, sacrificed so much. Let's build, together. But you cannot keep traveling for the company and working for NSU. It's killing you. The kids and I miss you, and you miss us. Why have we made these tremendous sacrifices if we don't get to spend time together?"

"You are correct, this is not our path forward. I figured that being a professor would give us a stable life. I'm scared that if I leave the safety of salary and job security, then I will be the guy who had a chance to be a good provider and failed because of selfish ambition. I know what poverty is, and I don't want that for our family. Besides, I sense my time as a professor has grown only more irksome, while my time growing our business, doing the hard work of helping people become their best self, that's where my heart is. I love it."

"I get that, I really do. If there is anyone in the world that I'd bet on, it's you—and us. We're gonna make it. Believe!" Two times before I had sacrificed money, title, and career to forge ahead like an 1860s American pioneer headed westward under the promise of the Homestead Act to lay claim to land and future. The stakes were higher than at any other time in our lives, given two dramatically different paths.

"I'd bet on me too. Always have. Always will."

As I got in my car and tried to figure out where next to go, a voice called from somewhere deep in my soul, "Meet me in

Rehoboth. We have got some talking to do." God was calling me to the very place where we met at other crossroads in my life.

I must have looked like a deranged lunatic on that beach, in March, in my shorts and sandals, freezing my ass off, yelling up at the clouds for hours on end. God and I walked together, from Rehoboth to Dewey Beach and back, spending hours together as my toes became numb and my fingers lost their feeling. "Here is your home, where you will build a life with your family. Come home."

Upon my return, I recounted to Kristen my "Scenes from an Asylum" walk with God. Before getting to the conclusion of my newly formed grand plan, she piped up with her usual supernatural foresight—as she had done previously before I was able to blurt out "I'm gonna get a PhD."

"We should move to Delaware. Remember when we were on Ski Hill Road, dreaming of building our company in either Key West or in Rehoboth Beach. That was our original idea. Somehow, in all the schooling and hurdles and baby making, we strayed off the path. Let's go to the place where we got married, and raise our family, build our business, and make a life." It was time to pivot.

Within months of relocating to Delaware, I found myself again on the boardwalk of Rehoboth Beach, desperately seeking how to gracefully exit my position as acting department chair and professor, stop traveling for speaker keynotes and workshops, and realize our original plan to create a hotel that could be used as a vacationer's paradise, a corporate retreat center, and a place for wellness and yoga retreats. This time, the only way forward was to leap.

I called my friend and realtor. "Yo brother. How about you find me a hotel to buy?" I proceeded to lay out the vision for our company: "A lifetime of coastal vacations and retreats."

"I got the place," he said, immediately setting up a showing at the Canalside Inn, located within walking distance of the beach, situated sidelong next to water, at the highest point in city limits. With thirteen rooms, holding up to thirty-seven guests, and a downstairs kitchen and socializing areas perfectly appointed for groups and families, Canalside Inn was the perfect place for us to bring our dreams into reality.

Ideally located just three hours from Baltimore and Washington, DC, and two hours from Philadelphia, Rehoboth is a short drive from a gazillion people and companies. At this location, we could completely flip our business model: Instead of me flying to every corner of the world to speak, clients will retreat at the Canalside Inn, where I can facilitate retreats in paradise. This was the solution that would give us a stable revenue stream from beach travelers, keep me off the speakers' circuit, give us freedom and flexibility to raise our family according to our schedule, and travel as a family.

Buying Canalside Inn, leaving my job as a professor, and becoming entrepreneurs was the logical conclusion of everything Kristen and I had worked for since we met. Building our leadership development company from scratch gave us the tools and business know-how to quickly operationalize and rebrand the hotel. Our experiences in the spring break and travel industry gave us a working knowledge of how to negotiate contracts and work as hoteliers. Our time learning to run our burgeoning training company taught us how to be nimble, innovative, and pivot quickly away from what doesn't work to invest time, money, and effort into what does work. From the moment we took the reins of Canalside Inn, we implemented the business plan we concocted on a long and snowy walk in Leavenworth.

## WHY YOU SHOULD CARE ABOUT BUILDING
## ENTREPRENEURIAL MUSCLE

On the path that led me to entrepreneurship, every decision, every struggle, every moment of doubt and triumph, was a rep in building my entrepreneurial muscle. Living an entrepreneurial mindset and building entrepreneurial skills isn't just about business acumen; it's about discovering how you can add value to the world, solve problems that no one else can, build belief in yourself and your abilities, nurture resilience, and see opportunities where others see obstacles.

The sleepless nights spent agonizing over research papers, the gut-wrenching decision to leave the security of academia, the fear of failing my family—these weren't just challenges to overcome. They were the resistance training that strengthened my entrepreneurial fiber. Each experience was a protein-rich meal for my developing business mind, nourishing my growth and preparing me for the rigors of entrepreneurship.

Research shows that entrepreneurial leadership is not an innate trait but a skill that can be developed over time.[77] Like any muscle, it requires consistent exercise and proper nutrition to grow. The "exercises" come in the form of calculated risks, innovative problem-solving, and relentless pursuit of a vision. The "nutrition" is derived from a voracious appetite for learning, the wisdom of mentors, and the hard-earned lessons of both successes and failures.

When entrepreneurs onboard employees, the goal is to have those employees follow your lead, to act as intrapreneurs. Intrapreneurship is the phenomenon that occurs when employees in an organization take on an entrepreneurial mindset, acting, thinking, and aligning their values with the organization as though they were the owners—effectively acting as the founder entrepreneur. Within established organizations, leaders can act as "intrapreneurs," driving innovation and creating new business opportunities. Intrapreneurs identify unmet needs, develop creative solutions, and take calculated risks to drive growth and improve the organization.

As I navigated the tumultuous waters of starting a business while juggling family responsibilities and academic pursuits, I was unknowingly engaging in what is known as "entrepreneurship practice"—a process of learning by doing that is crucial for developing entrepreneurial competencies.[78] Each pitch to potential investors, each workshop delivered, each strategic pivot was an opportunity to flex and strengthen my entrepreneurial muscles.

The emotional toll of this journey cannot be overstated. There were moments of crippling self-doubt, nights spent questioning whether I was selfishly pursuing a dream at the expense of my family's stability. My drive to help others, to make a tangible difference in people's lives, became the fuel that powered my entrepreneurial workouts. This aligns with research that suggests prosocial motivation is a key driver of entrepreneurial persistence.[79] Every time I saw a light bulb moment in a workshop participant's eyes or received feedback about how our programs had transformed someone's approach to leadership, it reinforced my commitment to this path.

The sacrifices were real and often painful. Giving up a stable income, uprooting our family, pouring our savings into a dream—these decisions weren't made lightly. But as Sarasvathy posits in her theory of effectuation, entrepreneurs often operate with a "bird in hand" principle, leveraging their existing means to create new ends.[80] We were using every resource at our disposal—our knowledge, our network, our passion—to build something meaningful.

Building entrepreneurial muscle isn't just about personal gain; it is about creating "shared value" for others and contributing to the greater good with social progress.[81]

As I share this journey, my hope is that you, the reader, will recognize the potential within yourself to build your own entrepreneurial muscle. Whether you are contemplating starting a business, leading a team within a larger organization, or simply seeking to inject more innovation into your daily life, the principles remain the same. Embrace challenges as opportunities for growth. Seek out knowledge voraciously. Take calculated risks.

Remember, every decision you make, every risk you take, every failure you learn from is another rep in your entrepreneurial workout routine. The input you receive from mentors, books, experiences—both good and bad—is the nutrition that fuels your growth. As you build this muscle, you will find yourself more resilient, more adaptable, and more capable of creating positive change in the world.

So, I challenge you: Start your entrepreneurial workout today. Embrace the discomfort, relish the learning, and remember that every step forward, no matter how small, is strengthening your capacity to lead, innovate, and make a difference. The world needs more people willing to take this journey, build businesses of their own, act like intrapreneurs when working for someone else, and lead with purpose.

# 11

## FINALE

When COVID-19 struck my mother in late 2020, our family knew how serious a health problem she was facing. At seventy-three years old, she was a breast cancer survivor with three separate hip replacements, a knee replacement, half a shoulder replacement, and diverticulitis. Mom's body had taken a lifetime of wear and tear from standing behind hair stylist chairs and bars serving drinks.

Mom said, "I am in the hospital with COVID-19. They ran out of beds in the emergency room so they put me in the intensive care unit (ICU)." *What? Hospitals don't shuffle people into the ICU because they run out of beds. Something else must be going on.*

"What's going on with Mom?" I said to Mom's husband.

"Your mom is on a ventilator and medicine. COVID-19 is really putting her down. She's having a hard time breathing. Doctors said she needs to be in the ICU because she is in critical condition."

A couple weeks later, Mom was released from the hospital, permanently in need of an inhaler. She had survived the respiratory symptoms, but COVID-19 led to worsening symptoms including congestive heart failure. Mom died in June 2022.

Mom was broken down by unloving parents and suffered tremendously from insecurities that she was never loved.

She vowed to herself to make her children always feel loved and powered through her life's challenges to give us a life better than her own. She was a mother who never stopped telling me how much she believed in me as a human full of potential. I gave my level best to test her belief in my goodness, and though we had many difficult moments in our relationship, her unwavering love prevailed. I never made it easy, but she allowed me the freedom to grow as a person without being a helicopter parent, to build a life of my making without trying too much to mold me in her image. Her love gave me inspiration to be better, and the confidence to know that when I failed, she would be there to help me pick up the pieces.

I think a lot about how parents are leaders, how parents are responsible for giving their children the love, attention, care, guidance, and space to become their future best selves. I ponder how parents are learning the ropes of "how to be a parent" while doing the best they can in that all important role. How parents fail, and get mad when kids act "bad," and then parents and kids learn to learn from one another.

Leaders similarly must accept their own failures, the fragility of their role in followers' lives, and the temporal aspect of being adored in one moment and despised in the next. Leaders must learn the ropes of "how to lead" while they are equally committed to performing the day-to-day operations of their roles.

The most valuable things parents and leaders can do is exactly what my mom did for me: Believe in the people who are in your care, support them as they grow, let them be wild and free under gentle guidance and direction setting, reassure them that no matter how "bad" they "fail," that you as a parent/leader will catch them and lift them up.

Mom bore witness in real time or heard tell of nearly

every story recounted in this book. These are my life stories, my lived experiences that transformed me into an authentic person and leader. A lot of these moments probably precipitated her heart problems, but she was always there to let me know that good and bad are parts of life, that all experiences shape the people we are and who we are to become.

I realize these events shaped who I am. I do not hide from my history, rather I raise it as a flag of my true colors. My history is as real as the six-inch scar that adorns my left cheek. My rough-around-the-edges, tough, and independent spirit are born of battles on the playground and skirmishes throughout my life. And yours are too, and everyone else's.

We are all the sum of our lived experiences, positive, negative, and everything in between. We can no more run from the past than we can hide from the changing image that stares back at us in the mirror. We can choose, though, how our past and present influence our future.

Take the lead in your own life. Hang out the window and throw out some newspapers that break windows and pivot toward a better you and a brighter future. Climb a mountain and look over a body of water to get a proper reflection of where you were and where you can go. Spend time listening to the silence. Allow yourself the space away from people and in nature to dive inside yourself to reveal your hidden truths, for that is when the epiphany will break through the noise of your busy life. Live. Learn. Lead.

Your lived experiences, intermingled among your ability to enjoy the good and not be overly burdened by the bad, inform your sense of self, the collection of identities you call forward and roles you play. A person's self-construct is highly complex and consists of idiosyncratic personality traits, goals, values, and character strengths and weaknesses.

Character strengths provide the resources within a person to make them more functional, effective, and high performing across a wide domain of roles they enact in their life. Character weaknesses foster negative self-view, self-defeating behaviors, insecurities, and other detrimental behaviors that cause a person to be less than fully functional, less satisfied, and force undesirable personal and professional outcomes. Choose to honor your positive self-aspects and character strengths; cherish your loved ones and followers. Choose to forgive yourself for those parts of your history that you don't like and the negative character aspects that you want to change about yourself. Endure the struggle to improve aspects of yourself that aren't as perfect as you prefer, because you are worth the struggle.

Our personal history, experiences, knowledge, and attributes contribute to what the mind perceives as a singular, unifying, representative, and total "self." The brain simply develops ideas about how our personal journey can be formed into a self-narrative that defines what it would like to be expressed as, "Who I am!" I dare say that who you are is a leader. Life bears out this fact. Science and data prove the theory that, yes, leaders are born. And, through reflection on the experiences of your life and investment in your personal development, you were made a leader. Simply stated, leaders are born to be made.

Developing leaders is so important, I dedicate my life to it. I chose to sacrifice my careers and corner offices, quit multiple six-figure salary jobs, and go back to school to earn an MBA and PhD in leadership and management. I made it my mission to transform today's ordinary citizen into tomorrow's leaders, and to always be a lifelong learner (as everyone should be). As a scholar and researcher, I have studied leaders, leading, and leadership for over a decade of reading and writing for peer-reviewed journals, speaking to academics and executives alike, and hosting corporate and wellness retreats. I have come to find that all the research in the world tells the same story—that a leader is a person, leading is an activity that can be taught and learned, and leadership is a relationship between a leader and follower. When conceptualized in this way, it is easy to see that anyone can be a leader at any time.

In my roles as entrepreneur, consultant, professor, and speaker, I tell C-suite executives, presidents, managers, and anyone who will listen, really, that I believe everyone is capable of leading. Without fail, whenever those words leave my lips, someone in the audience rolls their eyes, another groans, and without a millisecond of contemplation the doubting Thomases whisper to their neighbor a snarky cynical ridicule of the idea that all people can lead.

I know this is coming. I'm prepared for the inevitable land mine of questions that follow a statement that challenges people's existing mental frameworks and understanding of the natural order of things.

"Not everyone can lead," the skeptics shout, glued to what their personal experiences form in their minds as truth. "Some people don't want to lead. They are happy working their shift and going home, not ruffling any feathers, and putting their head down to get through the workday."

But these folks miss the point because they frame leadership as existing at work only, not recognizing that leaders live in every nook and cranny of everyday life. Every family has a leader. Religious organizations have leaders. Schools and governments have leaders. Leadership exists in civic associations and homeowners' associations. The military has leaders at every level of every unit. Kids play "follow the leader" on playgrounds.

Leaders are everywhere; their efforts often go unnoticed and unrewarded. Seriously, have you ever thought to thank a school crossing guard for leading children safely across the street? Biology, training and development, personal history and education, timing, and context influence leader emergence, and so I remind the naysayers that I believe that everyone is *capable of leading*, not that everyone *will lead*.

I believe, through witness and scientific validation, with every fiber of my heart, mind, and soul, that every person at every stage of life is capable of being a leader. At minimum, every human is capable of self-leadership, which makes them a leader of one—and that's the goal, to make the world a better place, one person, one leader at a time.

As a professor, I witnessed students start their leadership journey with low confidence in their leader abilities and then storm across the commencement stage years later during graduation ceremonies, proud as a peacock, after hearing their name called, knowing they have invested in themselves to acquire the knowledge, skills, abilities, and motivation to lead.

As a leader in companies, I have witnessed "natural born leaders" take charge as if it were their God-given right, and maybe it was. Similarly, I have seen people who have never led a day in their life step up when their team needed them most and found that leading suited them better than they expected. These situations provide a catalyst for leading, an impetus they never knew existed that stimulates internal motivation to lead. If and when that happens, they may lead in that moment and never lead again—but lead they did and *call them leader we must*.

I acknowledge with absolute certainty that some people will neither lead nor are they motivated in any way to be a leader. Their mental block to approaching leader roles is largely caused by the way people conceptualize what it means to be a leader, who leaders are, where they come from, what leaders do, and how leadership occurs in real life. Leaders and leadership do not exist in a vacuum of time and space. Leading is not about *being in charge* of people or a company and is not a superpower reserved for extraordinary people. Being a leader, and living a good life, is an accessible possibility for everyone.

Leaders coordinate and collaborate to achieve shared objectives, and intentionally develop followers. Authentic leaders practice being a leader by living a personal and professional life worth following—a feat that I have been challenged to achieve. Being a leader is simply one element of a lived experience, one identity called forth in contextually relevant situations.

Being a leader is to be in—or be selected for—a role where one can behave and think as a leader. To say that everyone is capable of leading recognizes the innate strength of the human spirit that exists within us all. Some folks call forward their leader identity, tap into their leadership spirit, and pull from within themselves their wealth of internal resources to live a life of leadership, whereas others do not.

Lucky for me that my two children teach me more about becoming a leader than did a combined three decades of leading in organizations and studying books. One day my three-year-old son and I were in Alaska picking wild salmonberries. Salmonberries grow in bushes about five feet tall. Now Gordon was about two-and-a-half feet tall at the time. I was picking berries and handing them down to him. When we had picked as many berries as I could see from my vantage point, I told Gordon it was time to move on. But he kept pointing saying, "berries, berries." I quickly told him there were no more berries. After his persistence, I got down to his level to tell him that he was wrong. Only, when I got down to his level, I was looking at about fifty juicy berries. Literally, the low hanging fruit.

We can learn from people of all ages so long as we are willing to see things from their perspective. Looking down, I could see no berries, but looking up from Gordon's vantage point, the bush was full of salmonberries. Here I was thinking I was leading him, and it turns out he was leading me.

Leaders are made in these moments, where the natural course of simply *being* and *doing* is, without effort or afore-thought, *leading*. All people who are young in spirit and willing to learn and be better, our children, and generations of people struggling to just make it through the end of each day, are the low hanging fruit as prospects for developing future leaders. Make them believe in themselves. Believe in yourself. You can lead. You are a leader.

Now, I have written this book with the purpose to help you see the leader within yourself, and to let you know that just because you may not be leading at present, when your time to lead does come, you know within yourself that you are ready—and then: *Jump! Jump! Jump* as high as you can, with all your might, with all the energy, confidence, and self-effi-cacy endowed upon your spirit!

For when that moment comes, your belief in your ability to lead will be so high, and your self-knowledge and self-love will be so strong, that you recognize *your moment* to *lead*, and throw yourself into the cause. Never mind the fact that you may not like being a leader and may choose to never lead again. The point is not how often or how long you lead; it is that you become aware your capacity for leadership is real and tangible. How you choose to enter and exit the role of leader is less important than the awakening that you must experience to call forth your powerful leader-self—your authentic and unique leader-identity.

Remember that a rising tide lifts all ships. People who learn to lead make everyone around them better. As we develop and invest ourselves in others, we grow and advance in our own leadership. We transfer those skills to our personal lives, to lead our families, to be civic leaders, and to be leaders in our religious institutions, sports leagues, academic clubs, parent-teacher associations, companies—any group or organization that we are a part of.

Imagine how much better off we would all be if everyone pulled out the leader from within themselves: people of all ages, ethnicities, and cultures everywhere in the world. I invested ten years of my life writing this book to invest in you and your leadership journey. And now, you have invested time and effort to read it and use it as an instrument for self-acceleration.

I have shared my pain, successes, joys, near death experiences, my highest and lowest moments, and divulged research and best practices acquired over a lifetime, for the purpose of pulling out the leader from within one person at a time. My goal in sharing my history with you is to encourage you to lead, because if I can lead, then you can lead.

I hope that you see a bit of yourself in these stories. We are all brothers and sisters, living the shared human leadership experience. I revealed my struggles, opened myself up and bared my soul, told you of my difficult climb, was vulnerable enough to acknowledge that I am not in any sense of the word a "natural born leader" and yet, I became a leader, a good husband, father, son, community member, business owner, and changer of lives.

I want you to know that no matter how bad you feel about yourself and your history, you are not alone. I am here with you, to be a guide that encourages you to leap into living well and leading positively.

As I said in my TEDx Talk, "You matter. You can lead. And your leadership matters. Say to yourself, 'Leading is something everyone can do. I am a leader!'"

# APPENDIX A

## ACKNOWLEDGMENTS

To my dear friend and mentor, Dr. Ethlyn Williams. You once said to me, "I'm willing to invest as much energy into your development as you are willing to put into your own development. Do not ever let there come a time when my caring for your success is more than your own caring for your own success." To this day, I hold myself and others accountable to this very high bar.

To my publisher, Henry DeVries. My deepest appreciation for your friendship. Thank you for pulling the best nuggets out of my brain and using them to explain complicated concepts in simple ways. Your guidance positively changed my life and our business.

# APPENDIX B

## ABOUT THE AUTHOR

Dr. Bryan Deptula is a leadership authority, author, speaker, CEO of BKD Leaders (a strategic leadership development and training company), and owner of Canalside Inn.

As an executive coach and corporate trainer, Bryan facilitates strategic planning for organizations and creates best practice leader development programs that work by improving individual and team performance.

Dr. Deptula values developing leaders who:

- *learn* to be their best self
- *lead* from within
- *live* with purpose

Bryan envisions a world where every person believes in their ability to lead, and 100 percent of the workforce is engaged and performs beyond expectations.

His mission is to improve the life and leadership of all people. Dr. Deptula achieves his mission by delivering dynamic keynotes, engaging workshops, and life-changing retreats. His leadership development programs build leader identity and brand, leader intelligence, and Leader M.U.S.C.L.E.

Bryan's TEDx Talk, "Leaders Are Born To Be Made," gives practical wisdom about how to make leaders out of all people while coordinating and collaborating to get work done with and through others. You can find his inspirational TEDx Talk at:

https://TED.com/talks/bryan_deptula_leaders_are_born
_to_be_made

Dr. Bryan Deptula's remarkable journey started in New Castle, Delaware, where he overcame childhood poverty to become a PhD, MBA, hotelier, Vistage speaker, and former university associate professor and management department chair at NSU's College of Business. Bryan's journey has taken him to over thirty countries spanning five continents, where he is a trusted advisor to executives, and has given thousands of keynotes, retreats, and workshops at conferences, government agencies, small businesses, and Fortune 100 global companies.

Bryan's work with executives, entrepreneurs, and companies across industries, small and large, has lead him to believe that today's greatest challenges are to help weak leaders become strong so they get the most out of a postpandemic, multigenerational, digitally-driven workforce that has zero attention span and commitment to employers, demands remote work and work-life balance, and needs emotional coddling and constant recognition. Our leader M.U.S.C.L.E.S. are weak because we are forced to use skills, styles, and approaches that we never needed and never used. As leaders, we don't know who we are, don't recognize our workforce, and nearly everything we knew about leading no longer works.

Dr. Bryan's keynotes and workshops are required learning because he gives the wisdom, knowledge, and power to shortcut a lifetime of learning to lead. He makes leadership, psychology, and organizational behavior research accessible through telling real life stories that reveal best practices to become a leader worth following. It's a narrative of overcoming inner struggles on the road to personal and professional development, intertwining authentic stories with research that offers you low-risk, high-reward strategies for making executives and managers better leaders.

Every keynote and workshop elaborates leadership lessons

that everyday people can understand and that are grounded in the science of learning to be your best self, leading from within, and living with purpose. Personal reflections and questions prompt participants to apply these insights to their own experiences and to practice leading by implementing the exercises and wisdom to improve their life and leadership.

Dr. Deptula's Leader M.U.S.C.L.E. model is the key to accelerating your life, business, and brand for emerging and experienced leaders seeking guidance to build themselves into a leader worth following and entrepreneurs creating a future by building a business.

Dr. Deptula has coauthored a combined twenty journal articles and conference presentations and authored a best-selling book. *Leaders Are Born To Be Made*, offers low-risk/high-reward strategies to make executives and managers better leaders. His book is a heartfelt gift to his children, offering invaluable life lessons to help them discover the leader within.

Dr. Bryan and his wife Kristen own the Canalside Inn (www.thecanalsideinn.com) in Rehoboth Beach, a many times Best of Delaware winner, where they host vacationers and corporate retreats.

Dr. Deptula possesses a unique talent for solving complex organizational puzzles, inspiring positive change, and transforming organizations. His unwavering commitment to guiding individuals toward their best selves and enhancing organizational leadership continues to make a profound impact on those fortunate enough to work with him.

Bryan shares practical wisdom on:
- *www.BryanDeptula.com*
- YouTube, Facebook, LinkedIn, and Instagram
  - @bryandeptulaPhD

## LEADERS ARE BORN TO BE MADE

To inquire about workshops, retreats, and bulk copies of this book, please email bryan@bryandeptula.com.

# APPENDIX C

## WORKS CITED

1    Bruce J. Avolio, James B. Avey, and David Quisenberry, "Estimating Return on Leadership Development Investment," *The Leadership Quarterly* 21, no. 4 (2010): 633–44.

2    Edgar F. Borgatta, Robert F. Bales, and Arthur S. Couch, "Some Findings Relevant to the Great Man Theory of Leadership," *American Sociological Review* 19, no. 6 (1954), 755–9, https://doi.org/10.2307/2087923.

3    Robert G. Lord, Roseanne J. Foti, and Christy L. De Vader, "A Test of Leadership Categorization Theory: Internal Structure, Information Processing, and Leadership Perceptions," *Organizational Behavior and Human Performance* 34, no. 3 (1984): 343–78.

4    Lynn R. Offermann, John K. Kennedy Jr., and Philip W. Wirtz, "Implicit Leadership Theories: Content, Structure, and Generalizability," *The Leadership Quarterly* 5, no. 1 (1994): 43–58.

5    Jan-Emmanuel De Neve, Slava Mikhaylov, Christopher T. Dawes, Nicholas A. Christakis, and James H. Fowler, "Born to Lead? A Twin Design and Genetic Association Study of Leadership Role Occupancy," *The Leadership Quarterly* 24, no. 1 (2013): 45–60.

6    Sankalp Chaturvedi, Michael J. Zyphur, Richard D. Arvey, Bruce J. Avolio, and Gerry Larsson, "The Heritability of Emergent Leadership: Age and Gender as Moderating Factors," *The Leadership Quarterly* 23, no. 2 (2012): 219–32.

7    D. Day, M. M. Harrison, and S. M. Halpin, eds., "Leader Development and Leadership Process," Special issue, *The Leadership Quarterly* 22, no. 3 (2011).

8    Bruce J. Avolio and Gretchen R. Vogelgesang, "Beginnings Matter in Genuine Leadership Development," in *Early Development and Leadership: Building the Next Generation of Leaders*, eds. Susan E. Murphy and Rebecca J. Reichard (Routledge, 2011), 179–204.

9    D. Scott DeRue and Susan J. Ashford, "Who Will Lead and Who Will Follow? A Social Process of Leadership Identity Construction in Organizations," *Academy of Management Review* 35, no. 4 (2010): 627–47.

10   Kim-Yin Chan and Fritz Drasgow, "Toward a Theory of Individual Differences and Leadership : Understanding the Motivation to Lead," Journal of Applied Psychology 86, no. 3 (2001), 481–98.

11   John Gowlett, *Ascent to Civilization: The Archaeology of Early Humans* (McGraw-Hill College, 1992).

12   Michelle Hammond, Rachel Clapp-Smith, and Michael Palanski, "Beyond (Just) the Workplace: A Theory of Leader Development Across Multiple Domains," *The Academy of Management Review*, 42, no. 3 (2017), 481–98.

13   Darja Miscenko, Hannes Guenter, and David V. Day, "Am I a Leader? Examining Leader Identity Development Over Time," *The Leadership Quarterly* 28, no. 5 (2017): 605–20.

14   K. Wehrle and U. Fasbender, "Self-Concept," in *Encyclopedia of Personality and Individual Differences,* eds. Virgil Zeigler-Hill and Todd K. Shackelford, (Springer Nature, 2020).

15   Norm Smallwood and Dave Ulrich, "Building a Leadership Brand," *Harvard Business Review* 85, no. 7–8 (2007): 92–100.

16   Cristiano L. Guarana and B. Avolio, "Unpacking Psychological Ownership: How Transactional and Transformational Leaders Motivate Ownership," *Journal of Leadership & Organizational Studies* 29, no. 1 (2022): 96–114.

17   D. Scott DeRue and Susan J. Ashford, "Who Will Lead and Who Will Follow? A Social Process of Leadership Identity Construction in Organizations," Academy of Management Review 35, no. 4 (2010), 627–47.

18   Christopher P. Neck, Charles C. Manz, and Jeffrey D. Houghton, *Self-Leadership: The Definitive Guide to Personal Excellence,* 2nd ed. (Sage Publications, 2020).

19   Jeffrey D. Houghton and Christopher P. Neck, "The Revised Self-Leadership Questionnaire: Testing a Hierarchical Factor Structure for Self-Leadership," *Journal of Managerial Psychology* 17, no. 8 (2002): 672–91.

20   Charles C. Manz and Henry P. Sims Jr., *The New SuperLeadership: Leading Others to Lead Themselves* (Berrett-Koehler, 2001).

21   Charles C. Manz and Christopher P. Neck, *Mastering Self-Leadership: Empowering Yourself for Personal Excellence,* 2nd ed. (Prentice Hall, 1998).

22   Christopher P. Neck and Jeffrey D. Houghton, "Two De-
     cades of Self-Leadership Theory and Research: Past
     Developments, Present Trends, and Future Possibilities,"
     *Journal of Managerial Psychology* 21, no. 4 (2006): 270–95.

23   Giacomo Rizzolatti and Laila Craighero, "The Mir-
     ror-Neuron System," *Annual Review of Neuroscience* 27
     (2004): 169–92.

24   David A. Waldman and Pierre A. Balthazard, "Neurosci-
     ence of Leadership," in *Organizational Neuroscience* (Em-
     erald Group, 2015), 189–211.

25   Richard E. Boyatzis, Melvin L. Smith, and Nancy Blaize,
     "Developing Sustainable Leaders Through Coaching
     and Compassion," *Academy of Management Learning &
     Education* 5, no. 1 (2006): 8–24.

26   Michael B. Harari, Ethlyn A. Williams, Stephanie L.
     Castro, and Katarina K. Brant, "Self-Leadership: A Meta-
     Analysis of Over Two Decades of Research," *Journal
     of Occupational and Organizational Psychology* 94, no. 4
     (2021): 890–923.

27   Joyce E. Bono and Timothy A. Judge, "Personality and
     Transformational and Transactional Leadership: A
     Meta-Analysis," *Journal of Applied Psychology* 89, no. 5
     (2004): 901–10.

28   Bernard M. Bass and Bruce J. Avolio, *Improving Organi-
     zational Effectiveness Through Transformational Leader-
     ship* (Sage Publications, 1994).

29   Bernard M. Bass and Ruth Bass, *The Bass Handbook of
     Leadership: Theory, Research, and Managerial Applica-
     tions*, 4th ed. (Simon and Schuster, 2008).

30 Bernard M. Bass and Bruce J. Avolio, Improving Organizational Effectiveness Through Transformational Leadership (Sage Publications, 1994).

31 Amy F.T. Arnsten, "Stress Signalling Pathways That Impair Prefrontal Cortex Structure and Function," *Nature Reviews Neuroscience* 10, no. 6 (2009): 410–22.

32 Lívea Dornela Godoy, Matheus Teixeira Rossignoli, Polianna Delfino-Pereira, Norberto Garcia-Cairasco, and Eduardo Henrique de Lima Umeoka, "A Comprehensive Overview on Stress Neurobiology: Basic Concepts and Clinical Implications," *Frontiers in Behavioral Neuroscience* 12 (2018): 127.

33 Sally S. Dickerson and Margaret E. Kemeny, "Acute Stressors and Cortisol Responses: A Theoretical Integration and Synthesis of Laboratory Research," *Psychological Bulletin* 130, no. 3 (2004): 355–91.

34 Ethlyn A. Williams, Rajnandini Pillai, Bryan Deptula, and Kevin B. Lowe, "The Effects of Crisis, Cynicism About Change, and Value Congruence on Perceptions of Authentic Leadership and Attributed Charisma in the 2008 Presidential Election," *The Leadership Quarterly* 23, no. 3 (2012): 324–41.

35 Robert J. House and Jane M. Howell, "Personality and Charismatic Leadership," *The Leadership Quarterly* 3, no. 2 (1992): 81–108.

36 Ethlyn A. Williams, Rajnandini Pillai, Bryan Deptula, Kevin B. Lowe, and Kate McCombs, "Did Charisma 'Trump' Narcissism In 2016? Leader Narcissism, Attributed Charisma, Value Congruence and Voter Choice," *Personality and Individual Differences* 130 (2018): 11–7.

37   Robert J. House and Jane M. Howell, "Personality and Charismatic Leadership," The Leadership Quarterly 3, no. 2 (1992), 81–108.

38   Robert K. Greenleaf, *The Power of Servant Leadership*, ed. (Berrett-Koehler, 1998).

39   Bruce M. Meglino and Elizabeth C. Ravlin, "Individual Values in Organizations: Concepts, Controversies, and Research," *Journal of Management* 24, no. 3 (1998): 351–89, https://doi.org/10.1016/S0149-2063(99)80065-8.

40   Jörg Sydow, Georg Schreyögg, and Jochen Koch, "Organizational Path Dependence: Opening the Black Box," *Academy of Management Review* 34, no. 4 (2009) 689–709.

41   Paul Schrodt, Paul L. Witt, and Amber S. Messersmith, "A Meta-Analytical Review of Family Communication Patterns and Their Associations with Information Processing, Behavioral, And Psychosocial Outcomes," *Communication Monographs* 75, no. 3 (2008): 248–69.

42   Tena Vukasović and Denis Bratko, "Heritability of Personality: A Meta-Analysis of Behavior Genetic Studies," *Psychological Bulletin* 141, no. 4 (2015): 769–85.

43   Bruce S. McEwen, "Neurobiological and Systemic Effects of Chronic Stress," *Chronic Stress* 1 (2017), https://doi.org/10.1177/2470547017692328.

44   Chris Argyris, *Integrating the Individual and the Organization* (Routledge, 2017).

45   Carston K.W. De Dreu and Laurie R. Weingart, "Task Versus Relationship Conflict, Team Performance, and Team Member Satisfaction: A Meta-Analysis," *Journal of Applied Psychology* 88, no. 4 (2003): 741–49.

46   Lindred L. Greer and Jennifer E. Dannals, "Conflict in Teams," in *The Wiley Blackwell Handbook of the Psychology of Team Working and Collaborative Processes*, eds. Eduardo Salas, Ramón Rico, and Jonathan Passmore (Wiley, 2017), 317–43.

47   Ralph H. Kilmann and Kenneth W. Thomas, "Developing a Forced-Choice Measure of Conflict-Handling Behavior: The 'Mode' Instrument," *Educational and Psychological Measurement* 37, no. 2 (1977): 309–25.

48   Jim Collins, *Good to Great: Why Some Companies Make the Leap...And Others Don't* (Harper Business, 2001).

49   Daniel Goleman, *Emotional Intelligence: Why It Can Matter More than IQ* (Bloomsbury, 1995).

50   Bruce J. Avolio, James B. Avey, and David Quisenberry, "Estimating Return on Leadership Development Investment," *The Leadership Quarterly* 21, no. 4 (2010): 633–44.

51   Christine D. Hegstad and Rose Mary Wentling, "The Development and Maintenance of Exemplary Formal Mentoring Programs in Fortune 500 Companies," *Human Resource Development Quarterly* 15, no. 4 (2004): 421–48.

52   David Megginson and David Clutterbuck, *Techniques for Coaching and Mentoring* (Routledge, 2004).

53   Terri A. Scandura and Ethlyn A. Williams, "Mentoring and Transformational Leadership: The Role of Supervisory Career Mentoring," *Journal of Vocational Behavior* 65, no. 3 (2004): 448–68.

54   Kathy E. Kram, *Mentoring at Work: Developmental Relationships in Organizational Life* (University Press of America, 1985).

55  Richard D. Cotton, Yan Shen, and Reut Livne-Tarandach, "On Becoming Extraordinary: The Content and Structure of the Developmental Networks of Major League Baseball Hall of Famers," *Academy of Management Journal* 54, no. 1 (2011): 15–46.

56  Bryan Deptula and Ethlyn Williams, "An Intersubjective Perspective on the Role of Communal Sharing in Synergistic Co-mentoring: Implications for Human Resource Development," *Human Resource Development Quarterly* 28, no. 3 (2017): 369–400.

57  Tammy D. Allen, Lillian T. Eby, Mark L. Poteet, Elizabeth Lentz, and Lizzette Lima, "Career Benefits Associated with Mentoring for Protégés: A Meta-Analysis," *Journal of Applied Psychology* 89, no. 1 (2004): 127–36.

58  Jon P. Briscoe, Stephanie C. Henagan, James P. Burton, and Wendy M. Murphy, "Coping with an Insecure Employment Environment: The Differing Roles of Protean and Boundaryless Career Orientations," *Journal of Vocational Behavior* 80, no. 2 (2012): 308–16.

59  Rajashi Ghosh, Wendy Marcinkus Murphy, Richard D. Cotton, and Kathy Kram, "Seeking Support from Multiple Developers: Assessing Optimal Structure, Content, Antecedents, and Outcomes of Developmental Networks," In *HRD Perspectives on Developmental Relationships: Research, Practice and Challenges*, edited by Rajashi Ghosh and Holly M. Hutchins (Palgrave Macmillan, 2022), 467–99.

60  Kathy E. Kram, *Mentoring at Work: Developmental Relationships in Organizational Life* (University Press of America, 1985).

61  John P. Kotter, *Leading Change* (Harvard Business School Press, 1996).

62  Kathy E. Kram, *Mentoring at Work: Developmental Relationships in Organizational Life* (University Press of America, 1985).

63  James B. Avey, Rebecca J. Reichard, Fred Luthans, and Ketan H. Mhatre, "Meta-Analysis of the Impact of Positive Psychological Capital on Employee Attitudes, Behaviors, and Performance," *Human Resource Development Quarterly* 22, no. 2 (2011): 127–52.

64  Paul J. Zak, "The Neuroscience of Trust: Management Behaviors that Foster Employee Engagement," *Harvard Business Review* 95, no. 1 (2017): 84–90.

65  Suzanne Dikker, Lu Wan, Ido Davidesco, Lisa Kaggen, Matthias Oostrik, James McClintock, et al. "Brain-to-Brain Synchrony Tracks Real-World Dynamic Group Interactions in the Classroom," *Current Biology* 27, no. 9 (2017): 1375–80.

66  Chris D. Frith and Uta Frith, "The Neural Basis of Mentalizing," *Neuron* 50, no. 4 (2006): 531–4.

67  Louis Cozolino and A. Santos, *The Neuroscience of Human Relationships: Attachment and the Brain* (New York: W. W. Norton & Company, 2014).

68  Roger E Beaty, Mathias Benedek, Robin W Wilkins, Emanuel Jauk, Andreas Fink, Paul J Silvia, Donald A Hodges, Karl Koschutnig, Aljoscha C Neubauer. "Creativity and the default network: A functional connectivity analysis of the creative brain at rest," *Neuropsychologia* 64 (2014): 92-98.

69 Marcus E. Raichle, "The Brain's Default Mode Network," *Annual Review of Neuroscience* 38 (2015): 433–47.

70 Giacomo Rizzolatti and Laila Craighero, "The Mirror-Neuron System," Annual Review of Neuroscience 27 (2004), 169–92.

71 Naomi P. Friedman and Trevor W. Robbins. "The role of prefrontal cortex in cognitive control and executive function," *Neuropsychopharmacology* 47(1) 2022: 72–89.

72 Tammy Allen, Lillian Eby, Mark Poteet, Elizabeth Lentz, Lizzette Lima. "Career Benefits Associated With Mentoring for Proteges: A Meta-Analysis." *Journal of Applied Psychology* 89(1) (2004), 127–36.

73 Anthony C. Klotz, Brian W. Swider, Yidou Shao, and Melanie Prengler, "The Paths from Insider to Outsider: A Review of Employee Exit Transitions," *Human Resource Management* 60, no. 1 (2021): 119–44.

74 Sumita Raghuram, N. Sharon Hill, Jennifer L. Gibbs, and Likoebe M. Maruping, "Virtual Work: Bridging Research Clusters," *Academy of Management Annals* 13, no. 1 (2018): https://doi.org/10.5465/annals.2017.0020.

75 Julie Tetzlaff, Gwen Lomberk, Heather M. Smith, Himanshu Agrawal, Dawn H. Siegel, and Jennifer N. Apps, "Adapting Mentoring in Times of Crisis: What We Learned from COVID-19," *Academic Psychiatry* 46, no. 6 (2022): 774–9.

76 Lori Allen Ford and Bryan Deptula, "The Wage Gap: No One's Responsibility, But Everyone's Problem," *Compensation & Benefits Review* 51, no. 3 (2019): 112–28.

77  Donald F. Kuratko, "Entrepreneurial Leadership in the 21st Century," *Journal of Leadership & Organizational Studies* 13, no. 4 (2007): 1–11.

78  Charles C. Manz and Christopher P. Neck, Mastering Self-Leadership: Empowering Yourself for Personal Excellence, 2nd ed. (Prentice-Hall, 1998).

79  Toyah L. Miller, Matthew G. Grimes, Jeffery S. McMullen, and Timothy J. Vogus, "Venturing for Others with Heart and Head: How Compassion Encourages Social Entrepreneurship," *Academy of Management Review* 37, no. 4 (2012): 616–40.

80  Saras D. Sarasvathy, "The Entrepreneurial Firm," in *Handbook on Organisational Entrepreneurship*, ed. Daniel Hjorth (Edward Elgar, 2012), 193–207.

81  Michael E. Porter and Mark R. Kramer, "Creating Shared Value: How to Reinvent Capitalism—And Unleash a Wave of Innovation and Growth," *Harvard Business Review* 89, no. 1–2 (2011): 62–77.

# INDEX

# INDEX

## INDEX